THE
VIRGINIANS

Books by Michael Edelhart

COLLEGE KNOWLEDGE
LIVING ON A SHOESTRING
INTERFERON: NEW HOPE FOR CANCER
THE HANDBOOK OF EARTH SHELTER DESIGN
THE VIRGINIANS

THE VIRGINIANS

Michael Edelhart

Principal photographs by
LEE BRAUER AND THOMAS DANIEL

Doubleday & Company, Inc., Garden City, New York
1982

DESIGNED BY LAURENCE ALEXANDER

ISBN: 0-385-15773-8
Library of Congress Catalog Card Number 80-2048
Copyright © 1982 by Michael Edelhart

Contents

Introduction

Virginia, mother of Presidents. Virginia, the state for lovers. Virginia, cradle of democracy, home of the First Families, bond between the Blue Ridge and the sea, Capital of the Confederacy.

Virginia is a paradox, caught on the cusp between North and South, past and future, mountain and ocean, city and farm. Packed within the bounds of this commodious commonwealth is all the variety of terrain, life-styles and attitude that comprises the national spirit.

The Old Dominion represents a unique distillate of American experience. It ranges from extensive bays and ocean beaches through some of the lushest green hills in the world to ancient, rocky, coal-laden mountains, from the nineteenth century ruralness of Appalachian hollow dwellers to the twenty-first century housing developments and the problems of that urban corridor that snakes southward from Washington, D.C. Even the state's commerce reflects this quintessential quality: Virginia's three biggest enterprises are those all-American staples, tobacco, tourism and U. S. Government.

Virginia is a state with deeply rooted traditions. While the Commonwealth is experiencing the urban ills, energy problems, labor strife and economic woes common everywhere, it is with a subtly different spirit. Virginia's old-time gentility remains. The faint trace of faith in her native aristocracy lingers. And the fair-dealing optimism of a newly minted America still imbues her perspective and actions. The commonwealth stands poised on the edge of change, with one hand tenaciously reaching back toward the past.

From the earliest American settlements—Virginia boasts both the first successful settlement, Jamestown, and the longest continuous community, Hampton—Virginia has been seminal to the nation's development. And this pre-eminence has made an unmistakable mark on the Virginia character.

One essential fact to keep in mind, when thinking about Virginia attitudes, is that in America's formative years, Virginia and America were virtually synonymous terms. Geographically, old Virginia extended from Cape Henry, where the original settlers landed, through what is now Kentucky and Tennessee, all the way to the edges of the Middle West.

As Virginia Moore pointed out in *Virginia Is a State of Mind:* "Physically, Virginia has shrunk, the better part of five states having been amputated from her: Maryland, North Carolina, Kentucky, Tennessee and West Virginia—to say nothing of the District of Columbia. Lopped off like arms and legs. But the torso remains, and the heart is in the torso."

Thomas Jefferson's famous book, *Notes on Virginia,* isn't really about the state. It makes the natural assumption, for a Virginian, that any discussion of the commonwealth automatically encompasses the entire nation. Jefferson spent as much time talking about the notion of America in the book as he did on the details of the commonwealth.

Historically, early Virginia produced the men and ideas that created the American democracy. Because it also served as the site for many of the most vital events in the nation's formation, it has been said that "Virginia is the main street of American history."

And culturally, Virginia "created the one genuine aristocracy which this country has known or is likely to know. But she did not create it because her pioneer settlers were the offspring of a dull English nobility. The aristocracy grew out of the conditions of life— out of the very soil and climate. That was what made it legitimate, powerful and unique," according to Agnes Rothery.

The casual sense of importance, of specialness, engendered in those colonial days still remains an important element of the Virginia self-image. Virginians do not brag as wildly or openly about their state as do other Southerners. This is not because they have less to crow about, but because it would be unseemly for a person in so utterly favorable a circumstance to belabor the obvious to less-fortunate individuals. The Virginian, supreme in confidence, answers wild-eyed boasts with silence and a smile.

"We Virginians," wrote Pulitzer Prize-winner Virginius Dabney, "modestly admit our superiority to citizens of all other American states. We can handle a Northerner without half trying, whether it be inside the squared circle, at the brass rail, or with derringers at ten paces."

An even more sweeping statement of Virginia's divine position came from Thomas Nelson Page, who said at a Jamestown Celebration in 1907: "It has been well said that God acts through His prepared agencies; that He prepared Virginia to place the seal of

His favor on, and the Virginia colonists and their successors as His instruments to accomplish His mighty work."

Even a Virginian might admit that such a characterization is stretching things a bit, but just a bit. Divine anointment aside, the sense of greatness inherent in being a Virginian has given the condition enormous cachet. A person from a large city in the Middle West may consider himself a Chicagoan. Dwellers in other areas may identify themselves primarily as Americans or as members of an ethnic group. But denizens of the Old Dominion think of themselves of Virginians first. U. S. citizenship is a pleasant by-product of the more cherished citizenship of their native state.

At times, Virginia citizenship has seemed so desirable that people have adopted it for themselves in the face of all logic and reality. Once, when General Douglas MacArthur, an Arkansan, was asked about his origins, he didn't say, "I'm from Arkansas." That would simply not have been fitting for the American Caesar. Instead, he announced: "It was intended that I be born in Virginia, my mother's home." MacArthur was not about to let a petty detail like geography confuse his true origins.

A similar case is Edgar Allan Poe, who has been claimed as a native, it seems, by every state on the Eastern Seaboard. He was born in Boston. Lived in New York. Died in Baltimore. But, on the strength of a few years passed in Richmond, he stated: "I am a Virginian, or at least I call myself one."

New residents of the Old Dominion succumb to Virginia identification rapidly.

"I am a Virginian," they announce within weeks of moving in.

"But you lived in New Jersey for thirty-five years!" long-time residents protest.

"Well, I was born in New Jersey. But now I'm a Virginian," the adoptee insists. In fact, like a religious convert, the newly arrived Virginian soon becomes a zealot for all things native. He can only be distinguished from home-grown Virginians by the radiating intensity of his citizenship.

No other state has this effect on its population to so large an extent.

Another buttress to Virginians' self-satisfaction is certainly the breathtaking physical variety and beauty of their state. Even its outline on a map is suggestive of something unique: a plumed arrow pointed straight toward the heart of America.

Back in 1606, a recruitment poem by Michael Drayton lured potential colonists with these lines:

> And cheerfully at sea,
> Success you still entice,
> To get the pearl and gold,
> And ours to hold
> Virginia,
> Earth's only paradise.

And, when the colonists arrived, they sent glowing reports home. "Take the four best kingdoms of Christendom, and put them all together," wrote Governor Sir Thomas Dale to King James in 1611, "and they may in no way compare to this country."

Captain John Smith rhapsodized that "Heaven and earth never agreed better to frame a place for man's habitation. Here are hills, plains, valleys, rivers and brooks, all running most pleasantly into a faire bay encompassed about with fruitful and delightsome land."

Unfortunately, life in Virginia's first settlements wasn't always as delightsome as it was billed. "Our men were destroyed with cruell diseases and Swellings, Flixes, Burning Fevers and by warres," wrote George Percy from Jamestown, "and some departed suddenly, but for the most part they died of meere famine. There were never Englishmen left in a foreigne country in such misery as wee were in this new discovered Virginia."

Still, the land in Virginia was astonishingly fruitful, and despite all the early hardships, settlers continued to come. The society they carved out slowly began to approximate the pie-eyed descriptions of the Virginia Company's early hucksters. In 1788, Thomas Jefferson wrote his friend Angelica Church that "I have been planning what I would shew you: a flower here, a tree there; yonder a grove, near it a fountain; on this side a hill, on that a river. Indeed, madam, I know nothing so charming as our own country."

And the tendency remains lively today. Just a few years ago, Guy Friddell gushed: "In the sweet undulating roll of Virginia you can catch the soft folds of the Blue Ridge Mountains in the morning

mist, the giddy, gaudy green Easter egg hills blowing around Albemarle, the lazy James embracing Richmond, the dark green tobacco fields somnolent in the South-side sun and the long pale green combers rolling in white thunder on Virginia Beach."

Indeed, Virginia does encompass within its boundaries an unmatched variety of physical splendor. Utah may have greater mountains; Hawaii may have more spectacular beaches; Texas may have more overwhelming sweeps of plain; New York may have more hurly-burly. But Virginia has it all.

From the broad, smooth beaches of Virginia Beach, the state flows gently upward along the network of Chesapeake tributaries. Norfolk, Hampton, Newport News. Towns of fishermen, shipbuilders, sailors. Birthplace of American colonization.

At the fall line, the James River passes Richmond, the heartland of the Confederacy, and becomes one of the most interesting white-water rapids in the East.

Make a right turn at Richmond and you head up the flat, strong shoulder of the Piedmont. You cross the Matta, Po and Ni rivers, which gave the Mattaponi Indians their name. You cross Spotsylvania where Alex Haley's ancestor, Kunta Kinte, suffered in slavery. You pass innumerable creeks and inlets from the spreading Potomac River. And in time you reach northern Virginia, the second ganglion of the East Coast megalopolis.

Turn left when you hit the traffic jam backing up from Washington and you'll enter the quiet, pastoral horse country. Rolling green hills hold storybook estates. Gingerbready houses stand among the white-fenced paddocks and green-brown fields.

Shortly you will reach the Blue Ridge. Ahead lies Harpers Ferry, described by Jefferson as "worth the trip from Europe" of its own accord. The hills are a green so dark it verges on purple, and the sky abandons its customary wan blue for a richer, smokier shade.

Meander south along the hills. The humpback summits grow steadily higher, the valleys deeper and longer and darker. You come upon the sinuous, smooth banked Shenandoah River, named by the Indians "daughter of the stars." In the nooks around the river valley lie hot springs that bubble with health, and legendary caves that writhe beneath the surface, rioting with stalactite and stalagmite color. Over yonder you can see the Natural Bridge. Jefferson considered it so singular a natural formation that he wangled a way to own it. Washington shinnied up the side and carved a colonial graffito in the side. It has been described as a site that looks as though it was designed by the white man and constructed by the Indians.

Gazing down toward the distant point of the Virginia arrowhead you can see the second range of mountains, the Allegheny, curving toward Tennessee. And if you look back toward your left, you can see the hills falling away behind Roanoke, carrying downward the rivers that water the Piedmont fields, and pass the historical cities on their way home to Chesapeake Bay and the sea.

A Virginian is but a few hours removed from any kind of American experience he can think of. He can go to a fiddler's convention. Or deep sea fishing. He can commune with his ancestors or ride the futuristic Metro. He can ski in the mountains or lie on the beach. He can hear at least a dozen distinct American dialects and vocabularies and visit towns whose cultures have changed little since the 1700s. Or, he can spend his time in cities and suburbs that were but a gleam in a developer's eye ten years ago.

It is, in short, a unique and superlative environment. Virginians feel privileged to live there. They have a greater respect for what they get from their surroundings than most people and a consequent greater love for their home. Living in such magnificent surroundings, who wouldn't feel a certain smugness?

Customarily, people who live in the midst of bounty take great pleasure in food and drink. Virginians embrace this trait with gusto. In colonial days, Governor Sir William Berkeley set the tone when he characterized Virginia as "the land of good eating, good drinking, stout men and pretty women."

The prized Virginia foods are ham and bacon. Not any old ham and bacon, but Virginia ham and bacon. George Bagby had the definitive word on this subject: "The only perfect bacon and the only perfect greens are found in Virginia. And hence it follows, as the night the day, not that the Virginians are the only perfect people, but that they are a peculiar and very remarkable people."

The degree with which these people enjoyed their libations flabbergasted that stiff Englishman Charles Dickens. On his trip through the state in 1842, he wrote that "the mounds of ice and the bowls of mint julep and cherry cobbler they make in these latitudes are refreshment never to be thought of afterwards, in summer, by those who would prefer contented minds."

Virginians, however, have thought of them often and for years, remaining remarkably contented all the while.

Because Virginians in all periods have been so pleased with the way things are, they have always been loath to see things change. They are not so much conservative in the rock-ribbed political sense as they are traditional. For this reason, Virginians have not often been the generators of new ideas. Rather, they have provided the crucible in which new-fangled notions cooked up elsewhere are fused to the traditional values of American life.

An example is the current inner-city renaissance in Richmond. Other areas may improve their dilapidated residential districts with massive, modern civic projects, but not Virginia. In Richmond the venerable Fan district is being restored by enthusiastic young couples using their own money. They are creating homes that retain the appearance of Civil War rowhouses—a trademark that lends the district its charm—but contain every modern convenience imaginable. Some of the new-old homes even have solar power. The result is a revitalized section that looks much as it did at its historical peak decades ago but functions in the most up-to-date fashion possible.

Virginia sees herself as the nation's conscience, frowning on extreme behavior in any direction, maintaining the national character in the safe, middle ground where it belongs. And, considering Virginia's unique position in American development, such a belief isn't as windily self-important as it might seem.

It has been said that the Virginia character is a good deal more British than American. For Virginians, the perfect state would be "to the manor born," specifically an English country estate. Today, with the thinning of regional characteristics everywhere, the British nature of true Virginianism has blurred. But as recently as 1956, the identification was near total, as this anecdote from the New York *Times* attests:

"We were invited to a dinner. Quite informal. Don't dress. And there at last was our beau ideal. His clothes, with just a faint echo of the Edwardian, were beautifully tailored. The gold watch and chain had obviously been his grandfather's. His linen was faultless. His English accent was what is now classified here as U (upper class) as opposed to non-U. We asked our host about him. "Oh,

9

George. Been here a couple of years, I believe. Comes from Virginia. Brilliant chap!"

Of course, for all the British names and affectations, Virginia never would have survived without settlers and citizens from many locales. Germans settled the Shenandoah Valley, bringing their language and devotion to work with them. Feisty Scots struggled into the hollows of the western hills, where they felled the trees and scooped the coal with determination. Hugenots, too, spiced the Virginia mix.

The result is a state view of life that is English in its affectations, German in its steadiness, discipline, and simplicity of worship, French in its subdued lust for the good things of life and Scottish in its wry humor and capacity for work. An altogether felicitous blending that has produced more notable personalities than any other in America.

While they may not be progressive, Virginians are anything but conformist. To the contrary, Virginia has long been a hotbed of fierce individualism. As Virginia Moore noted: "Virginians are the most unmitigated, incorrigible, thorough-going, unqualified, consummate, whole-hog, glaring, flagrant, enormous, fabulous, perfect, stark, radical, down right, pure, headlong, rampant, irregardless, tooth-and-nail, devil-may-care, bull-at-the-gate individualists in the world. If you don't know this, you will never know Virginians. It is the key to their character."

"Virginians," adds columnist James J. Kilpatrick, "as a breed put great store in privacy and the right to be left alone." This means left alone by outsiders, by unruly neighbors, by the state government and most of all the Federal Government.

Virginians, by and large, still reflect a Jeffersonian view of life. They can't understand why an American has to be pestered by his government. They hold to John Randolph's view that what America needs is as little government as it can get away with; a few laws, written in plain and simple language.

Jefferson's influence on the Virginia character, in fact, is certainly greater and more enduring than that of any individual on any other population in America. He abhorred any tie between church and state. Today, Virginia still will not hire chaplains for the state prisons because it involves religion; the religious denominations have to hire and pay the chaplains themselves.

Jefferson extolled the virtues of closeness with the land. "Those who toil on the earth," he said "are the chosen people of God." Virginians today, even city dwellers, hanker for a lot of ground to fool with. The state may be the most gardened area on earth. When economic conditions force farmers to take jobs in town, they hang onto their land and farm on the weekends. Some industries even give days off during harvest season to prevent worker revolts. Many a Virginian will put up with a smaller house to get a bigger yard. And many will willingly drive miles and miles to work so they can have a satisfactory swatch of country around their home.

Perhaps Jefferson's lingering influence explains why Virginia's ruralites differ from their counterparts around the South. A Virginia farmer or sharecropper may be poor, may be poorly educated, may be isolated from outside events and influences, but seldom is he shabby or ashamed.

As Marshall W. Fishwick has written: "Virginians, whether operating farms or motels, planting tobacco or working in steel mills, remain Virginians."

It's no surprise that Virginia gave birth to the image of the Waltons, rather than the commoner Southern stereotype of "The Beverly Hillbillies." Rural Virginia has been, and remains, a place of grace and quiet dignity through all the poverty and prejudice that have ravaged the land too many times.

It seems quite natural therefore, that Earl Hamner, imbued by this rural Virginia spirit, kept his family flame alive throughout his Hollywood career with such force that he could still recreate the world of his childhood on "The Waltons."

In Virginia it is easy to hearken back. But more and more there can be felt throughout the state an aching to move forward, too: cautiously, calmly, but steadily forward. A cauldron of change is beginning to bubble in the commonwealth.

Virginians now confront nuclear power. Slums. Pollution. Crowding. Cynicism. Lack of money and loss of tradition. In the generation ahead, the long-enduring Virginia style may succumb to the pressures of life in techno-America. Or it may rise, as it has so many times in the past, to show the rest of the nation how to meld the problems and opportunities of the present with the strengths and lessons of the past.

What is Virginia?

Virginia is the white-gloved lady at the Heart Fund Ball, and the begrimed coal miner blowing dust from his nose as he rises from the pit.

Virginia is the swaggering swabee at Newport News and the saucy teenager at an Alexandria disco.

Virginia is the fallen American soldiers at Arlington and his fallen Confederate ancestor at Richmond.

Virginia is the birthplace of Robert E. Lee and the home of Kunta Kinte.

Virginia is five grizzled old farmers lazing around a pot-bellied stove in Buckingham and a NASA test pilot at Langley.

Virginia is a seventy-year-old mountain woman with a burlap bag, her knees permanently bent from stooping to dig out wild ginseng, and an eighteen-year-old mechanic who dresses up on weekends to refight Civil War battles.

Virginia is the lean black preacher who towers over his pulpit and decries, "If the Lord loves you, then you must love yourself!" and the skinny sharecropper who sits on his steaming stoop at dusk to catch a hint of breeze.

Virginia is the land of Jefferson, of individualism and of gentility; a spot where, as Captain John Smith put it: "no extreame long continueth."

"Virginia," wrote George Bagby, "is a nation."

Ghosts
of the Past

" . . . The six and twentieth day of April [1606], about foure a clock in the morning, wee descried the Land of Virginia. The same day wee entred into the Bay of Chesupioc directly without any let or hinderance. There wee landed and discovered a little way, but wee could find nothing worth the speaking of, but faire meddows and goodly tall Trees, with such Fresh-waters running through the woods, as I was almost ravished at the first sight thereof. . . .

"The nine and twentieth day we set up a Crosse at Chesupioc Bay, and named that place Cape Henry. Thirtieth day, we came with our ships to Cape Comfort; where we saw five Savages running on the shoare. . . .

"The twelfth day [of May] we went backe to our ships, and discovered a point of Land, called Archers Hope, which was sufficient with a little labour to defend our selves against any Enemy. The soile was good and fruitfull, with excellent good Timber. . . . If it has not beene disliked because the ship could not ride neere the shoare, we had setted there to all the Collonies contentment.

"The thirteenth day, we came to our seating place in Pasiphas Countrey, some eight miles from the point of Land, which I made mention before: where our ships doe lie so neere the shoare that they are moored to the Trees in six fathom water.

"The fourteenth day, we landed all our men, which were set to worke about the fortification, and others some to watch and wars as it was convenient. . . .

"The fifteenth of June we had built and finished our Fort, which was triangle wise, having three Bulwarkes, at every corner, like a halfe Moone, and foure or five pieces of Artillerie mounted in them. We had made our selves sufficiently strong for these Savages. We had also sowne most of our Corne on two Mountaines. It sprang a mans height from the ground. . . ."

So did Master George Percy describe the beginning of Virginia history. In fact, the beginning of American history. A few ships, a few brave souls setting up the first community in the heart of what would shortly become the United States.

The cross that Percy's compatriots erected at Cape Henry still stands today. Peering from the monument's base up the inlet toward modern ↓ y Virginia is an eerie experience. From this spot the first white settlers stared at a verdant wilderness. Now, the signs of successful civilization are everywhere.

But the sensation of standing with the past radiates from the Cape Henry monument. You feel the grizzled, armored colonists standing on either side, looking upriver with you, bemused, amazed and proud of what had grown from their efforts. You feel bound up in events and emotions played out long ago.

There are spots all over Virginia where the visitor can feel such intimate ties with the past. Like an old house that has become so steeped in its own history that it veritably seems to speak, to breathe, the faded reality it has known.

Not ersatz tourist traps or overblown monuments, but genuine dedications to days gone by, often quite muted, even neglected, Virginia's historical heirlooms bespeak the incalculable contribution the commonwealth has made to American development. You might be wandering down a forest path when a leaf moved aside reveals the worn and wordless tombstone of a fallen Confederate soldier. At a stoplight in the heart of town you might casually glance at a small brass sign to discover that you are idling on a spot where Washington confronted the massed forces of the king. On a quiet small-town street you might come upon a huge house whose aura of age is so overpowering you know instantly it has seen at least five generations of Americans from cradle to grave. Testaments to the past don't have to be commercial and huge. In Virginia many are, and even more aren't. It is their ubiquity more than their size or notoriety that makes them so special.

Standing at Bull Run on a summer afternoon with the wind rustling the trees and the grass swaying in the sunshine, it is easy to hear the famous roar that saved the first battle of Bull Run for Stonewall Jackson and the Confederacy: "Let us determine to die here and we will conquer. There stands Jackson like a stone wall. Rally behind the Virginians!"

Upon leaving the dim interior of historical Stoner's Store in Fredricksburg, with its steep rows of odd-shaped apothecary jars, boxes of old-fashioned provender and quaintly dressed staff, you walk back out to the street and are startled to see cars and people in modern dress. You expect carriages, hoop skirts and high starched collars.

Watching the placid James River from the bow of the Haddon Ferry as the sinewy old ferryman poles you across the wide water, you nearly hear the paddles splashing from Indian canoes and the sibilant sad song of the slaves wafting from the fields.

Wandering about the grounds at Mount Vernon you find yourself staring oddly at the trees. After a time you realize you're trying to figure out *which* tree might be a descendant of the infamous chopped-down cherry.

Standing on a Shenandoah ridge, watching the thin blue river wind around the verdant hills, through the shadowed hollows, with an immense span of sky crowning the scene, you imagine the surge of awe that must have struck the first people to look on this place. It looks much the same now as then; it is breathtaking. How stunning it must have been to come upon the sight without expecting to find it!

The past in Virginia, though; doesn't just live in monuments and faded plaques to long-distant battles. It lives in the hearts of modern Virginians. Virginians have a penchant for commemoration and remembrance that isn't matched in America. They love to recreate the old ways, to wander in settings reminiscent of the past. Virginia is replete with ghosts of the past.

And Virginians have a unique interplay with their history. They dwell on it and draw on it. They are surrounded by it. They revel in it. It has been suggested that a Virginian's relationship with history is like an artist's with his colors. He dips into it, dabbles with it, uses it to highlight his life. And, as a painting contains all its colors but expands far beyond them, a Virginian's life is suffused with history but represents much more than a mere reliving of the past.

Virginians, said Guy Friddell, enjoy "a kind of double life in the living and the telling, shaping it to their ends, finding rich meaning and color in the clay of existence."

The basis for history's importance to Virginians is obvious. The state is stuffed with the raw material of history—remnants and relics of the past. It is literally impossible to drive for an hour on any major road in Virginia without passing a spot rich in American events. Historical markers line the highways, statues rise from every park. Birth places, death places, scenes of armistice and war overlap one another in a crazy quilt of significant happenings.

Consider: In Virginia, the first settlement in America was established. The first Presidents were born. The Declaration of Independence was written. Patrick Henry cried, "Give me liberty or give me death!" John Marshall established the precepts that still govern the conduct of the Supreme Court. The Revolutionary War's last battle was fought. So were the Civil War's first and last battles, along with more than one thousand in between.

The monuments of this rich legacy far surpass the offerings of any other state. Presidential houses are scattered in all directions. Historical graveyards are shadowed by the historical churches that accompany them. And plantations lie so thick about the countryside that the return of the South's great age appears quite plausible.

If the government put gates at the borders and charged fifty cents admission, Virginia would make a credible open-air museum.

But the core of Virginia's relationship with the past doesn't lie in the stone testaments. It transcends them, infusing every corner of Virginia landscape and every life. The sense of history touches the mundane and mighty events of Virginia today. Children go to school carrying a touch of the past. The state legislators rise to speak under the soft gaze of their predecessors. The softball players in the park, the lumbermen in the mountains, the ladies at the church social, the farmer in his fields go about their business with an unspoken and barely conscious nod to Virginia's past. The gentle dust of bygone days is sprinkled over the whole state and its inhabitants.

A sense of timelessness ensues from this feeling of kinship with forebears. Even transplants to Virginia from other states soon fall under the spell. After a few short months in the state they will speak of long-past events and people with the familiarity and fervor of kinfolk. Nowhere else in America does this magical interplay between then and now occur so pervasively.

Winston Churchill, a perceptive fellow, sensed the special quality of Virginia instantly, on a state visit here in 1930: "It takes only a few hours by train," he later wrote, "to go from Washington to Richmond, but we breathe a different air. It is another country . . . Mellow light plays around long-beleaguered valiantly defended, world famous Virginia. The hum of Chicago, the rattle of Wall Street, the roar of New York, the even tranquil prosperity of California, all are absent. We have entered the domain of history. We march with Lee and Jackson, with Stuart and Longstreet and with early autumn through woods lonely in their leafy splendors, old gold and fading crimson."

And historian Arnold Toynbee, a noted pessimist about

America, wrote that "Virginia makes the painful impression of a country living under a spell, in which time has stood still."

This is certainly not the case. Virginians aren't anchored by the past. A better image might be that they circle about it. As progress occurs, the circle grows ever larger, encompassing more experiences, but the center never changes and its influence on the changing circle remains constant.

This influence is deep. It has played a singularly important role in the formation of the Virginia character. As Marshall Fishwick noted: "Virginia is compounded of white supremacy, noblesse oblige, greatness, meanness, ancestor worship and the spell of a gloriously remembered past."

Douglas Southall Freeman once stated that Virginians are so focused upon the past that they practice "a mild form of Shintoism." And Virginius Dabney agreed, with the amendation on that "mild" might not be nearly a strong enough word. "The favorite indoor sport in Virginia," he said, "is still climbing about on the family tree."

But both men, and many other students of Virginia culture, have meant such comments as compliments, not chastisements. They see fascination with the past as enriching the Virginia heritage, as binding together generations and the disparate groups that comprise modern Virginia. Respect for history is like a fine sauce: not necessary, but deliciously enhancing.

Virginians express their interest in the past principally by spending a lot of time traveling around their state and visiting the historical sites it offers. Perhaps no other population in the country has such an interest in climbing over, touring or re-creating tangible images of its past.

And what is particularly special about Virginia is that the sensation of living history can arise on a downtown street corner or in the front of a run-down house in the older part of town as easily as at Monticello.

This is true because Virginians haven't merely memorialized their past, they've preserved it. Not satisfied simply to erect monuments and preserve famous houses, Virginians have frozen whole neighborhoods, even cities, in much the way they were years ago. And, where time has worn down fine old areas, Virginians have moved back in and restored them to their former finery. Woe betide the unfortunate developer who has challenged the forces of historical preservation in Virginia.

In Richmond, for instance, young professional families, college professors and artists have transformed the dilapidated Fan district into a marvel of post-Civil War beauty. The narrow, turreted houses line the shady streets with the defiant pride only genuine survivors can attain. Their refurbished interiors may be as modern as money can buy, but their exteriors remain faithfully antique.

In Alexandria, the entire downtown has been done over in the style of that city's heyday as a colonial port. In Old Towne Alexandria a modern pleasure-seeker finds the amusements of today housed in the fashion of yesterday. Old Towne succeeds in being soothing and exciting at the same time. No small achievement.

Virginians don't undertake these projects self-consciously. They do it because they sincerely like living in the old style, and they would hate to see it disappear. Even when Virginians build new homes, they go to great lengths to make them look like the traditional item. It's a point of honor in Virginia to combine modernity with reverence for the past.

This active re-creation of the past doesn't stop at houses and real estate. Virginians by the hundreds bring the past back as literally as possible in numerous reenactments of Revolutionary and Civil War battles. Virginians love to dress up on the weekend in the colors of their local regiment—or the accompanying feminine fashion—and take to the fields to replay the famous local altercation.

Accountants, gas jockeys, lawyers and garbage men don their tri-cornered hats or their Confederate caps, their breeches and boots, their greatcoats and rifles. They become transformed into spookily accurate images of their great-grandfathers. Then, with a gusto their bedraggled, underfed, cold and scared ancestors probably never achieved, they chase one another over hill and dale, blasting away with their flintlocks, igniting cannon fire, bellowing orders to the flanks and generally having a hell of a good time.

It is entertainment, but also tribal rite. The ritualistic union of today and yesterday. The message it carries loud and clear is: "Don't forget! Remember the past and keep it holy!" And Virginians do.

The apotheosis of Virginia's love affair with the past is Colonial Williamsburg. This fanatically realistic restoration of Virginia's first capital—complete with colonial foods, colonial craftspeople, colonial games, sports, music and accents—is a spectacular entertainment. It draws tourists as honey draws flies.

But Williamsburg represents something different for Virginians than it does for visitors from far away. The out-of-stater comes to Williamsburg and sees a vision of life as it once was. Quaint, historical, easy going. Williamsburg is a high-brow amusement park.

But the Virginian goes to Colonial Williamsburg and sees a vision of life as it still ought to be. Small scale. Richly centered on the land. Reasonably practical and reasonably pious. Williamsburg is an institutionalization of the Virginia ideal.

Consequently, Virginians feel more pride for Williamsburg than for anything else in the commonwealth. They can barely wait to hustle their visitors there for a visit. Alas, they are often disappointed that the folks from Toledo and Tucumcari don't see the significance of the place.

To express their native pride in Colonial Williamsburg, Virginians throw themselves into the task with a dedication and capability that overwhelms all disbelief. This vast historical charade requires live players—soldiers, sailors, butchers, bakers and candlestick makers. And the meticulous detail Williamsburgers bring to this recreation, coupled with the joy they radiate in doing it, creates the aura of total reality that makes it so unique. It takes Colonial Williamsburg out of the realm of amusement and into the higher sphere of anthropology.

Another of Virginia's spectacular re-creations of past glory is the First Thanksgiving celebration at Berkeley Plantation. This stems from the discovery by a Virginia historian of papers charging early Old Dominion colonists to celebrate a Thanksgiving Day each year. Immediately, Virginians leaped up and claimed the holiday as their own. The Pilgrims, it is claimed, merely copied a Virginia original.

In the spirit of state patriotism, the inheritors of the estate of Benjamin Harrison, a signer of the Declaration of Independence, began holding a full-dress replication of the first Thanksgiving as it would have been in colonial times. Heaping platters of game and turkey, enormous bowls of vegetables, crisp honeyed colonial sweets are carted through the baronial halls by hordes of volunteers in authentic dress. Sitting amid colonial trappings, eating colonial food, being served by colonial servants, it becomes impossible not to *feel* like a colonial scion. The heady sensation of the past remembered blurs the definition of reality and blends with the present. You almost expect Benjamin Harrison himself to rise, like Banquo's ghost, and address the party.

In fact, Virginia's residents from the past do include a number of ghosts who appear to modern folk from time to time. One of the most interesting of these is Lizzie Rowland, who lives in the mill house at Berkeley Plantation.

The house was built in 1849 by Spencer Rowland next to a mill he had refurbished for the Berkeley estate. Rowland lived in the tall angular house with his daughter, Elizabeth.

She was an only child and much beloved by her father, but her life was lonely. In her youth she had a lover who lived at a nearby plantation. In the stillness of the country nights he could often be heard for miles, galloping his steed along the paths toward Elizabeth's house. But the affair ended sadly, and Elizabeth died a spinster in 1870.

In the room where Lizzie died, her name is mysteriously etched into a windowpane. Many folks say this is the mark of Lizzie's ghost who has been seen now and again drifting through the house, peering out the windows toward the road, looking for her lost love.

Mrs. Grace Harrison, who lived in the house, talked about Lizzie's appearances: "As one drives or walks on a moonlight night, it is at times quite startling to see 'Miss Lizzie' standing at the side door or peering out of one of the windows. Sometimes if you stand still for a time this figure in white, which seems to have a light in her hand, will pass from one window to another. She has been seen a good many times in the past years and by quite a few people. I have heard my uncle, William Harrison, tell that on several occasions he was so certain someone was in the house he went all over it searching and calling. The ghost never roams when anyone is at home, but only when she has the place to herself. Possibly her Spirit is awakened by the hoofbeats on the road of some passing traveller."

The allure of the past casts its spell on new Virginians in short order. Recently arrived residents whose ancestors were picking potatoes in Poland or squabbling over kingly tithings in France while Williamsburg was in flower, soon speak of it in wholly personal tones. And wish they could return to a life they never came from.

Some say that Virginia's interest in the past has held it back in modern times. Dr. George Denny once quipped that: "It is a tradition that Virginia's motto 'Old Virginny Never Tires' is to be traced to the fact that Virginia habitually refuses to move fast enough to get tired."

Other wags noted, at the time of Virginia's recent Constitutional revampment, that the state was finally being dragged, kicking and screaming, into the nineteenth century.

But Virginius Dabney expresses the true situation better in his book *Virginia: The New Dominion:* "It is not the commonwealth that George Washington and Thomas Jefferson knew, nor yet that of Woodrow Wilson and Carter Glass. It retains many of the qualities that endeared it to those notable men, but it also is imbued with characteristics nowhere evident in the Virginia of their time. Some Virginians are nostalgic at this hour for the Old Dominion, and all of us must cherish and revere its virtues. But let us today salute the new dominion with its challenge and promise."

In other words, respect for the past doesn't stop Virginia's progress, it merely richens it.

Virginia's abiding interest in the past has brought about some unusual squabbles over the years, however.

Take, for instance, the case of poor General Dan Morgan, hero of the Civil War, who almost created another war in this century. Morgan is buried in Mt. Hebron Cemetery near Winchester. Twenty-nine years ago, a squad of South Carolinians tried to steal Dan Morgan's bones, on the pretext that his great-great-great-granddaughter lived thereabouts, so they had a right to him.

Winchester countered with a great-great-great-grandson of their own and refused to give Morgan up. The argument raged, with politicians weighing in on both sides, until a New Jersey historical society quietly noted that Morgan had originally come from New Jersey. He was a damn Yankee by birth! New Jersey offered gleefully to take him back to his native soil.

Faced with that prospect, the combatants settled. Virginia kept the bones, but put up a fancy new monument so the South Carolinians could go home feeling that they had done Dan Morgan a good turn.

Finally, one custom points up Virginia's unique reverence for the past better than all others combined. Ever since colonial days, when they signed a treaty giving up almost everything they had to white settlers, Virginia's Indians have been exempt from state taxes with the proviso that each fall they present the governor with a buck deer on the Capitol steps.

And every year, in full regalia, the Indians still present the governor with his buck. He soberly accepts it and announces that the Indians are exempt from taxes for one more year.

Is it an empty publicity stunt? Not really. It might have descended to that level elsewhere, but not in Virginia. Here, it's simply the faithful fulfilling of an old bargain. Nobody would ever consider stopping it, or changing the rules. A bargain remains a bargain no matter how long ago it occurred.

To fool with the agreements of the past would be simply unthinkable. To abandon or disrespect the good sense and courage that had come before would be sacrilege. It would be unnatural for Virginians to think otherwise.

Virginians do not play at the past. Their stance is utterly natural and unforced. Virginians stand at the edge of a historical wave, the current ripple in an unending continuum. They know better than any other Americans that the past never stops and the present never begins. They flow.

As a commonwealth history buff once said to me: "When you say the name Virginia, it reverberates back through time."

In Colonial Williamsburg living scenes can take on the timelessness of paintings.

The Hamners, the television family known as "The Waltons."

Ships, like tiny toys, search the vast ocean for fish as the sun rises.

Reading about history isn't enough for Virginians; they have to relive it.

The long locks of a young Virginian recall those of his great-grandfather.

The joy of a young couple in Williamsburg today is the same as it was two hundred years ago.

Robert Coles of Charlottesville bears an astonishing resemblance to his fifth generation ancestor, Thomas Jefferson.

Mrs. Gus Welch of Bedford, whose husband shared the gridiron with legendary Jim Thorpe.

Absorbed in his music, a fiddler at Williamsburg leads a dance.

A Waterford coppersmith maintains the look and art of a bygone time.

Changing the hour on The Miller School clock in Albemarle County has been done the same way for a hundred years.

First Family
Virginians

Virginia has long had a rather stiff upper crust, the First Families of Virginia. Traditionally, they have been the great landowners, well endowed, well educated. They lead lives of ease and view themselves as the natural leaders of their society. It was this sense that prompted John Adams' statement that "people in all nations are naturally divided into two sorts, the gentlemen and the simplemen. The gentlemen are generally those who are rich, and descended from families in public life." Although not a Virginian, Adams captured the sense of highmindedness and separateness that characterized the FFV:

"I am an aristocrat," said John Randolph, Virginian to the core. "I love liberty. I hate equality."

Early on the aristocratic nature of FFVism established Virginia as the preeminent American state. As Count Herman Keyserling noted, "The only real cultural atmosphere one finds today in America is that of Virginia. The cultured men who were born in its fields of force are responsible for most that is of cultural value in America. But how different Virginia is from all other states! Its culture a particular one; it is not a matter of age, but of kind as well."

This paramount position wasn't based upon mere inheritance, as it was for its aristocratic precursors in England; it came from a deep sense of leadership and public responsibility.

But the FFV tradition wasn't all stiff upper-lipped public service. William Caruthers, a significant romanticizer of the Virginia tradition, called FFVs "that generous, fox-hunting, wine-drinking, duelling and reckless race of men, which gives so distinct a character to Virginians wherever they may be found."

And Daniel Hundley, in his nineteenth-century study of southern social standards, said, "Scarcely has [the young Virginia gentleman] gotten fairly rid of his bib and tuckers before we find him mounted on horseback; and this is not a hobby horse either (which the poor little wallflower of the cities is so proud to straddle) but a genuine live pony. By the time he is five he rides well; and in a little while thereafter has a fowling piece put into his hands, and a little black boy of double his age up *en croupe* beside him. So accoutred, he sallies forth into the fields and pastures in search of adventures."

With all the talk of aristocracy and "cavalier" Virginians, it's easy to lose sight of the fact that the roots of FFVism lie in a rustic meritocracy, not a tradition of grand courts and ballrooms. "Most of the Virginians who counted themselves gentlemen were still, in reality, hardly more than superior farmers," wrote Wilbur J. Cash in *The Mind of the South*. "Many great property owners were still almost, if not quite, illiterate. Life in the greater part of the country was still more crude than not. The frontier still lent its tang to the manners of even the most advanced, all the young men who were presently to rule the Republic having been more or less shaped by it. And, as the emergence of Jeffersonian democracy from exactly this milieu testifies, rank had not generally hardened into caste."

While Cash's characterization might be overly harsh, it is true that the Virginia upper class was only a few generations removed from the middle class.

The Randolphs, as a case in point, were descended from William Randolph, who came over as the nephew of a merchant. William worked his whole life to acquire money and property. He studied law, worked with the colonial assembly, and built up a big enough stake to get some servants and land. Then he married into a socially prominent, landed family. Genuine nobility fell on his son, John, who was knighted by the king of England.

The heralded King Carter, whose holdings dwarfed just about everyone else's, who left his children more than 300,000 acres and a thousand slaves to divvy up, came over from England as a simple trader. His family, apparently, were wine merchants in London. Carter was far more a robber baron, a grasping capitalist, than any sort of Virginia gentleman. He created so much enmity in his lifetime of rough and tumble financial dealings, that a disgruntled compatriot scratched into his tombstone:

> Here lies Robin, but not Robin Hood
> Here lies Robin that never was good,
> Here lies Robin the God has forsaken
> Here lies Robin the Devil has taken.

But, as with the Randolphs, the second generation of Carters earned greater social prominence and had more leisure to attain "gentlemanly" status. "That Carter's acquisitive talents aroused no pride in later generations, looking back with different values," wrote King's biographer, is typical of any society's inheritors of a position which gives them a claim to aristocracy. As in the model of England,

A modern-day backwoodsman at National Monument State Park.

The Ruffin Tylers at their ancestral home, Sherwood Forest.

The master of the hunt calls the hounds to action.

Two generations of King Carter's descendants carry on the Virginia custom of opening the family estate to visitors. They host tours of Shirley plantation.

Virginians parade with fife and drum as they have for three hundred years.

The boys get down to some serious pickin' at Mabry's General Store.

A magnificent expanse of mountains provides the perfect spot for a picnic.

Deeply held religious faith and ritual characterizes the Amish and Mennonite residents of Virginia's mountains.

Hard mountain life can make faces as creased and weathered as stone.

Many Virginia blacks still live in poor, rural surroundings.

Pride in black heritage at a festival in Reston.

Menhaden fishermen gathering up the nets that hold their elusive quarries.

A boy and his crab will not soon be parted.

To retain closeness with the land, some Virginia farmers still employ dray horses for plowing.

A White Russian marked for death by the Reds, Mrs. Bergman fled to
Virginia to live peacefully on her small goat farm.

A weary soldier during training at Quantico.

it was essential for those born into social privilege to disassociate themselves from the acquisition of money. By their superiority to money, they implied some sort of mystic annointment in which their families had been elevated by God and King to a patrician status in a time so distant as to be beyond a beginning.

In such a fashion was the Virginia aristocracy born.

All the qualities of roughness and civility that paradoxically combined in the early FFVs are probably better exemplified by William Byrd II than by anyone else. Byrd spent much of his early life in England. He became immensely popular and garnered both social and political support and the genuine upper class polish that only England could produce at the time.

Byrd returned to Virginia when his father died. He inherited a prosperous holding in lands, fur and slaves, which he increased through innate shrewdness, a good nose for trends, and a better brain than any of his contemporaries. He became a delegate to the House of Burgesses and later to the more august Council of Virginia. He wrote one of the most influential books of the era, dabbled in science and built one of the first grand houses in the colonies.

But don't be lulled into thinking this was some pure-minded paragon of virtue. Byrd, for all his social training, was basically a raw, lusty frontiersman at heart. He chased women incessantly. His meticulously kept diary reveals a rough-hewn fellow who might make a modern Virginian blush.

Here is what he had to say about November 2, 1709:

"I rose at 6 o'clock and read a chapter in Hebrew and some Greek in Lucian. I said my prayers and ate milk for breakfast, and settled some accounts, and then went to court where we made an end of the business. We went to dinner about 4 o'clock, and I ate boiled beef again. In the evening, I went to Dr. b-r-t's where my wife came this afternoon. Here I found Mrs. Chiswell, my sister Custis, and other ladies. We sat and talked till about 11 o'clock, and then retired to our chambers. I played at (r-m) with Mrs. Chiswell and kissed her on the bed till she was angry and my wife also was uneasy about it, and cried as soon as the company was gone. I neglected to say my prayers, which I should not have done, because I ought to beg pardon for the lust I had for another man's wife. However, I had good health, good thoughts and good humor, thanks be to God Almighty."

Today, the FFV stratum remains intact. Its opulence is diminished. Its hold on Virginia education and government is weakened. But it persists in the right schools, the right clubs, the right neighborhoods and in the board rooms of Virginia's biggest companies.

But, what is an FFV?

An accurate, though tart description comes from Garrett Epps' novel, *The Shad Treatment,* when a character in the book recalls St. Cyprian's, a fictional, perfect FFV school. "St. Cyprian's did teach its students to be gentlemen as that term was defined in Virginia: special creatures for whom there may once have been a place in the universe, nineteenth-century petty squires who live close to the land without living off it, gentlemen farmers, hunters, fishermen, who made their livings dabbling in law or medicine or finance or real estate, rejoicing in their station in nature and society; the middle class of the great chain of being. The St. Cyprian's gentleman would never lie to, steal from or cheat his social equal, was unfailingly polite to ladies and helpful to idiots, maintained a proper but uncomprehending reverence for the Episcopal Church, a suspicious but unshakeable allegiance to the national government of the United States, a judicious fealty for the Apple-Farmer and his political organization and a moist-eyed worship for the memory of General Robert E. Lee."

Or as King Carter, a distant, colonial FFV relative of President Jimmy, noted, "It is not fine clothes nor a gay outsight, but learning and knowledge and virtue and wisdom that makes a man valuable."

And finally, a Massachusetts senator once said after a trip to Virginia: "They have an aptness for command which makes the Southern Gentleman, wherever he goes, not a peer only a prince. They have, the best of them, and the most of them inherited . . . the sense of duty and the instinct of honor as no other people on the face of the earth."

FFVism, then, means using one's position in a gentlemanly fashion for the good of society. Paternalistic as this attitude may be, it is far better than the sheer money-grubbing outlooks of the well-to-do in other areas. Only in Boston has anything similar to Virginia's civic-minded upper class ever developed in America.

The ultimate FFV, as Epps noted, was Robert E. Lee. Virginia Moore writes that in Lee "the best of Virginia had taken on flesh and blood." A scholar, statesman, gentleman, soldier and modest soul, Lee epitomized—and still does—all a Virginian could hope for in a personality.

He was born into a family illustrious from the earliest days of the colonies. The founder of the Lees of Virginia was Richard, who sailed for America in 1646. Later, Thomas Lee, his grandson, built the family seat, served as a burgess and later, sat on His Majesty's council for the colony. Thomas' six sons all served the colonies and the new country in important capacities. "A band of brothers," John Adams called them, "intrepid and unchangeable, who like the Greeks at Thermopylae stood in the gap, in the defence of their country from the first glimmering of the Revolution in the horizon, through all its rising light to its perfect day." Robert E. Lee's father was the renowned Lighthorse Harry Lee, who almost single-handedly put down the Whiskey Rebellion, served three times as Virginia's governor, and uttered the famous eulogy of George Washington: "First in war, first in peace and first in the hearts of his countrymen."

Lighthorse Harry also set a standard for Virginia fealty and presaged his son's tragedy with his deathbed words: "Virginia is my country, her I will obey, however lamentable the fate it subject me to."

Lee graduated from West Point in 1829. He served for a time as an army engineer, then as an officer in the Mexican War. After the war he superintended West Point. Later, he was the officer who put down John Brown's abortive raid against Harpers Ferry.

Lee was a superlative officer. He served the United States with distinction, and was even offered a field command in the Union Army by President Lincoln as the Civil War approached. But he found himself forced to make a wrenching choice between his loyalty to Virginia and his duty as an officer of the U. S. Army.

Lee's home sits on a ridge in Arlington overlooking the Potomac River and Washington, D.C. One can imagine him agonizing as he viewed one set of responsibilities out the front door and another, in Virginia, out the back.

What made Lee's decision even harder was that he had little sympathy with the slavery issue but felt secession was too extreme an action to take. Still, his intense loyalty to Virginia won out and he left the army to serve his native state.

Lee conducted himself through the Civil War as an exemplary soldier. He was perhaps not the greatest strategist—it has been said that his gentlemanly nature caused him to give in too easily to lesser minds rather than fight for his own superior ideas—but Lee sparked a phenomenal loyalty in his soldiers. It was for him, personally, that the Army of Northern Virginia fought so valiantly. It was his personality, his embodiment of the best the South had to offer, that kept the Confederate Army going as long as it did.

His surrender was impeccable. He went to General Grant dressed in a private's uniform, but with his jeweled Virginia sword at his side. He bargained until he won a strong surrender agreement for his troops, and left them, saying simply:

"Men, we have fought through the war together. I have done my best for you; my heart is too full to say more."

For all his achievements as a General, it is the grace of Lee's later years that truly sets him in the Virginia pantheon. Once the fighting was over Lee set himself with quiet diligence to the task of binding wounds and educating a new generation of Virginians not too badly scarred by the outcome of the war.

"Life is indeed gliding away," he wrote in 1866, "and I have nothing of good to show for mine that is past. I pray I may be spared to accomplish something for the benefit of mankind, and the honor of God."

To this end, Lee passed up many important jobs to take the presidency of small, poor Washington College. "I have a self-imposed task which I must accomplish," he said. "I have led the young men of the South in battle. I have seen many of them die on the field. I shall devote my remaining energies to training young men to do their duty in life."

At Washington, Lee set a hard but humane standard of conduct. There is the story of the tactful, but effective way Lee handled a lazy student who had taken to skipping classes.

"Sir," he said to the recalcitrant collegian, "I am glad to see you better."

"But General," the student replied, "I have not been sick."

"Ah," Lee said, "I took it for granted that nothing less than illness or distressing news could have kept you from your duty."

In another famous encounter with a student, Lee was forced to confront his own shortcoming, which he did with characteristic style.

"We do not want you to fail," said Lee to a sophomore, whose performance was edging toward the brink.

"But, sir, you failed," answered the student with thoughtless spunk.

"I hope," the college president replied evenly, "that you may be more fortunate than I."

It was the mix of bravery and humility and public service with private principles that made Lee the paragon Virginia figure. He accepted defeat in a way that made him grander for the losing. As Stephen Vincent Benét wrote:

> But there is nothing ruined in his face,
> And nothing beaten in those steady eyes.
> If he's grown old, it isn't like a man,
> It's more the way a river might grow old.

Charles Francis Adams, a Yankee, hailed Lee after the war by quoting Thomas Carlyle. These words better than any other explain Lee's position in Virginia lore:

> Whom shall we consecrate and set apart as one of
> our sacred men? Whom do you wish to resemble? Him you
> set on a high column, that all men looking at it may be con-
> tinually appraised of the duty you expect from them.

A note Lee once wrote, which was found after his death, points out the qualities that so endeared him to Virginians: "The gentleman does not needlessly and unnecessarily remind an offender of a wrong he may have committed against him. He cannot only forgive, he can forget. He strives for that nobleness of self and mildness of character which impart sufficient strength to let the past be but the past."

This is as good a statement of what Virginians strive for as any ever uttered. But the question of how successful they've been at achieving that goal remains open. Many a sharp-tongued rogue has taken potshots at Virginia's upper strata, claiming they aren't better people, merely snobs.

William Faulkner, while a visiting professor at the University of Virginia, countered these claims of FFV snobbery with the rejoinder, "I love Virginians because Virginians are all snobs, and I like snobs. A snob has to spend so much time being a snob that he has little time left to meddle with you." And Will Rogers weighed in with the comment that: "The Prince of Wales was born in Richmond—Richmond, England, of course. He didn't have enough ancestors to be born in Richmond, Virginia.

But the most vicious attack by far came from the acid pen of H. L. Mencken: "Consider the present estate and dignity of Virginia—in the great days indubitably the Premier American state, the mother of Presidents and statesmen, the home of the first American university worth the name, the *arbiter elegantarum* of the western world. Well, observe Virginia today. It is years since a first-rate man . . . has come out of it; it is years since an idea has come out of it. The old aristocracy went down the red gullet of war, the poor white trash are now in the saddle . . . A Washington or Jefferson dumped there by some act of God, would be denounced as a scoundrel and jailed overnight. Elegance, *esprit*, culture? Virginia has no art, no literature, no mind or aspiration of her own . . . In brief, an intellectual Gobi or Lapland. Urbanity; *politesse*, chivalry? It was in Virginia that they invented the device of searching for contraband whiskey in women's underwear."

Equally gifted voices, I must note, were raised in satire on the other side as well. Take these words of George Bagby, who wrote in the years after the Civil War:

> I know these Virginians pretty well. They are the greatest people on the face of the Earth. In fact, they are the only people. There was a time when, in my deep benightment and unloyalty to my ever dear old mother Virginia, I believed that Englishmen and Russians were people. Such, however, is not the case. I am wiser now and know that England is a country labouring under dry-rot. It is, as we Virginians say of a tree, "doted," and Englishmen are but the fungoid remains of what was once a people. It is not with much pleasure that I make this undeniable statement, for we of Virginia sprang from British loins. In like manner, the Goddess of Wisdom and of War sprang from that broken down old rake and thunderer Jove . . . As for Russians, they own slaves, and hence ape the manners of Virginians. But their slaves are white, and until they learn to say "thar" and to call a cucumber "curcumber" they cannot, in my opinion, lay any claim whatever to the honour of being called people.

Whew. One more waggish volley before moving on. In 1903
Harry Curran Wilbur wrote a syrupy poem called "In Virginia":

> The roses nowhere bloom so white
>   As in Virginia,
> The sunshine nowhere shines so bright
>   As in Virginia.
> The birds sing nowhere quite so sweet,
> And nowhere hearts so lightly beat,
> For heaven and earth both seem to meet
>   Down in Virginia.
> The days are never quite so long
>   As in Virginia,
> Nor quite so filled with happy song
>   As in Virginia;
> And when my time has come to die
> Just take me back and let me lie
> Close where the James goes rolling by—
>   Down in Virginia.
> There nowhere is a land so fair
>   As in Virginia,
> So full of joy, so free of care
>   As in Virginia;
> And I believe that Happy Land
> The Lord prepared for mortal man
> Is built exactly on the plan
>   Of Old Virginia.

Confronted by this smug assertion of Virginian superiority,
an anonymous Yankee penned this pithy response:

> Nowhere can toil so well suffice
>   As in Virginia,
> Nowhere ancestors cut such ice
>   As in Virginia.
> And I believe that lazy land
> Of fleas and niggers, heat and sand
> Is simply fashioned to be damned
>   In Old Virginia.

Leaving sarcasm aside, the standards of FFV conduct have
done much to keep Virginia business and politics on a high plane.

The famous response of William Battle to his 1969 gubernatorial defeat by Linwood Holton is a case in point.

Holton was the first Republican to win the Virginia state house in decades. As he was addressing his euphoric supporters on election eve, Holton stopped in amazement while regarding a condolence message to his opponent, when he saw that self same opponent striding through the crowd toward him.

"This is Virginia! This is Virginia, dammit!" squealed Republican Chairman Sam Carpenter gleefully as he accompanied Battle through the throng. That was the only explanation necessary for why Battle had come. It was Virginia. Let the past be but the past.

On the podium Battle raised Holton's hand and declared, "All the best, old boy!"

And on the way out of the hall, Battle responded to a newsman's question about why he'd gone out of his way to make the gesture by saying, "That was the only thing to do."

Apart from occasional high points like that, FFVism today is primarily a social distinction. The First Families have their clubs—particularly the Country Club of Virginia, whose very name says all you need to know about its attitudes—their private schools, their enclaves in Richmond, Tidewater and the horse country. They have their events—The Heart Fund Ball, the Bal du Bois debutante presentation, the Blessing of the Hounds. And their pastimes, the most popular being casual politics and chasing about the hills after foxes.

Now riding to the hounds, as this sport is called in Virginia, is a recreation that suits the commonwealth doyens right down to the polish on their riding boots. It is elegant, yet physical. Restrained, yet exciting. Countrified, yet refined. Riding is no small matter to upper-crust Virginians. Or as Fitzhugh Lee noted: "A Virginian teaches his sons to ride, shoot and tell the truth," The order tells the tale.

Head for any of the fine rural areas in the state—those expanses of spanking white barns set back from the road amidst cleanly manicured horse paddocks and crisp, checkerboard fields—during hunting season and you'll hear the toot of the hunt master's horn and his strange ululation as he calls the hounds. Park near an out-of-the-way intersection and wait. After a time you'll hear the distant thud of hooves and within minutes, the phalanx will rush by: flashing red coats and black tails, bright black boots, tan breeches, brown, grey and black horses cascading by in a flood of color and noise. Just as quickly they will be gone, crashing into the forest.

Stephen Vincent Benét captured the essence of an afternoon of riding to the hounds magnificently in his epic poem "John Brown's Body":

> The taste of ripe persimmons and sugar cane
> The cloy and waxy sweetness of magnolias . . .
> White cotton blowing like a fallen cloud,
> And foxhounds belling the Virginia hills.

Many modern-day FFV families work quite hard to maintain a life in line with the past. The lives of those who succeed remain remarkably like those of their grandfathers.

An excellent example are the Harrison Ruffin Tylers of Charles City County. Harrison and his wife, Fanny, still live at Sherwood Forest, the thirty-four-room, eighteenth-century manor where Harrison's granddad, President John Tyler, spent his days.

Harrison is a successful chemical engineer, and though his forebears would have made their living from the land, his homelife isn't too different from the family tradition.

The estate itself provides a magnificent olden-day setting for living the good life. The house sits amid 1,600 acres, all still held by the family. It is the largest frame structure in America, never more than one-room deep at any point. The furnishings are all original—not even period pieces brought in from outside to give a semblance of the past, but the real thing. It was owned by the family of President William Henry Harrison, before coming to the Tylers, the only known instance of one private house abiding two Presidents.

The modern-day Tylers still farm the estate, raising wheat, corn and soybeans. And, naturally, they raise thoroughbred horses for fox hunting. The three Tyler children all attended private schools and the University of Virginia, as have generations before them. Daughter Julia lettered at UVA in polo and is off in Corsica for adventure and seasoning. Eldest son, Ruffin, studies engineering at Jefferson's college, and younger son, William, is starting toward an architecture degree.

They are active, social, witty, polite people who absolutely delight in their strong valences with the past and with the easy, comfortable rural life they lead.

Another Virginian, a woman, lived out the FFV fantasy of aristocracy and public involvement in the ultimate fashion. Nancy Witcher Langhorne of Danville went over to England where she became Lady Astor. In 1919 she became the first woman ever to sit in the British Parliament. On that occasion, Winston Churchill grumped in public that it was "as though a woman had burst into my bathroom and I had nothing to defend myself with but a sponge." Lady Astor responded pungently, "Don't worry, Winston, you're not handsome enough to have worries of that kind." In 1922, when she returned to Virginia for the dedication of a memorial to her achievements, she said, "It is a strange thing that England's first female Member of Parliament should have come from England's colony." The inscription on her memorial cup read: "Behold, Virginia gives a daughter to her old mother."

In a speech in Staunton in 1912 Woodrow Wilson summed up the positive effects Virginia's aristocracy has had on the state's character rather well. In particular, his remarks explain why Virginia's aristocratic society has produced so many outstanding leaders:

> Men believe now that sooner or later their wrongs are going to be righted, and that a time is going to dawn when justice will be the average and usual thing in the administration of human affairs. . . . These standards were first established, so far as this side of the water is concerned, in Virginia. And no Virginian can stand up and look at the history of Virginia in the face and wonder about what the future is going to be. If I have any advantage as a Virginian, it is merely that I have a running start. A man that ties in with communities of this sort began further back, and the further back you got your start, the greater the momentum. All that is needed is the momentum. It does not need any cunning tongue. It does not need eloquence. It just needs the kind of serenity which enables you to steer by the stars, not the ground.

Joseph Bryan III and young Stuart, newspaper scions, with their wives by the family manse.

This rider's horse is more anxious to get started than she is.

State Senator Willy at his desk, the very picture of a proper, patrician Virginian.

An eager young horsewoman awaits the start of the hunt.

The Blessing of the Hounds at Cismont is one of the highlights of the hunt season.

Mountain Folk

The mountains are home to much of Virginia's lore and music. Life in the mountains is basic, religion fundamental, work hard and dangerous, and pleasures simple. Here the accents hearken back to the homelands, soft Virginia sounds tinged with Scottish brogue or German bark. And the lives, in these valleys shaded from the outside world, recall an older, easier time in American history.

The mountain people are a close-knit race, protective of their area and their lives. And who could blame them for trying to hold as their own a region described in these terms by an anonymous visitor from the 1900s:

"Any effort to convey to the reader the sensations experienced by the beholder would indeed be vain essay. . . . The sweep of the vision in every direction is unlimited, except by the curvature of the earth or the haziness of the atmosphere. The first idea suggested is that you are looking over a vast blue ocean, whose monstrous billows, once heaving and pitching in wild disorder, have been suddenly arrested by some overruling power."

Amazingly, it looks every bit as endless and breathtaking today as it did then. If you take Virginia Highway 55 from Washington, the view you see today as you enter the Shenandoah Valley is much the same as what John Lederer viewed three hundred years ago. The animals might have been wild, instead of domesticated farm beasts, the haze might have been more natural and less industrial, but the effect remains quite constant.

The people who live in this incredible scenic masterwork, shielded by the high, soft mountains, apart from the rest of the state in geography and background, have grown deeply close. They trust one another's reverence for the land of their ancestors. There is an unspoken, almost mystical bond between mountain people based upon a rich relationship with their mountains. They have an understanding of the needs of the place a non-dweller could never fully fathom.

Because of this trust, mountain people are extremely suspicious of strangers. They believe they live in paradise and don't want anybody coming in and messing it up. So, strangers often see the mountain folk as surly, ignorant and backward.

But among friends the mountaineers are loquacious, friendly and very funny. Their dry wit touches every conversation.

59

Mountain folk still sit around cracker barrels in old general stores up in the hills. They still ride tractors and pick-up trucks to small whitewashed churches on Sunday mornings. They still get together on Saturday nights to play fiddle and banjo on the porch while mosquitos buzz against the screens.

An old mountain curmudgeon once said to me, "There ain't nothin' outside these hills a man could want, nothin' outside these hills a man could need. They're as full of life, death, pain and happiness as any place in God's creation. These aren't rocks, they're livin' mountains."

Indeed, Virginia's mountains are alive—and contradictory. Superficially luscious, their underbelly holds scenes of darkness and danger as men moil for coal. They are blessed with natural abundance that serves to mask the economic poverty of many who live there.

If the first description of Virginia's mountains was rather contradictory, it seems to have been formulated with no reference to reality. Here is what an anonymous Jamestown colonist had to say about western Virginia: " . . . a dismal solitude or irremediate barrenness and perpetual gloom whose air was said to be infectious and mortal, the ground covered with serpents, the forests by wild beasts, and the indigenous inhabitants a race of fierce and brutal savages."

Despite the advance notices, settlers headed into the hills, which in reality were both beautiful and bountiful. These people were mainly Scotsmen and Germans, and today the preponderance of Germanic names and Scot accents can still be noted on any trip through the mountains.

The original mountain settlers were direct people not given to small talk or frippery, and today's mountain folk still are. In that, they are reminiscent of the people of Maine, or perhaps it's the other way around. In any case, a visitor who asks a mountain fellow for directions is likely to get back exactly what he asks for and not one bit more—and what he gets will come steeped in a heavy brogue.

> "How do I get to Fancy Gap?"
> "Eyou goo doon thee rood and to thee rah-eet."
> "Oh, how far down is the fork in the road?"
> "Aboot feh-eev maheels."
> "And how far do I go after getting on the second road?"
> "Until eyou git too Fancy Gap."

One reporter tells the tale of an early hiker on the Appalachian Trail who became lost in the Virginia hills. Wandering about, he saw the smoke of a mountain man's cabin. He scrambled down into the valley and approached the mountaineer, who eyed him suspiciously.

"How do I get down there?" the lost hiker asked, pointing.

The mountain man considered, then replied with finality. "Don't rightly know, son. I was born down hyar, ye know!"

The mountain people who are descended from tough Scotch-Irish and German stock worked their way up into these hills from the Piedmont or down from Pennsylvania, driven by poverty and a desire to live among their own kind rather than the dandified Englishmen of Tidewater. It took rough, unflinching people to challenge the physical rigors of the mountains and open up what at the time was stark wilderness. They were courageous, practical, religious folk, but simple in their personal lives and undesirous of commerce with "outside" areas even those within Virginia.

Daniel Boone is of this heritage, a man of enormous abilities and few words—who could handle the wilderness with aplomb, but lost his touch in civilized surroundings.

As a result, the mountain people were given short shrift by the river dwellers who ran Virginia. Even though the first major expedition into the Shenandoah Valley was led by a German, John Lederer in 1669, and an account of the expedition was authored by this "most ingenious person and a petty scholar," in the words of Sir William Talbott, Virginians downriver accorded the honor of first exploration to one of their own.

In 1716 Alexander Spotswood, Virginia's governor, led a beplumed and finely tailored band into Shenandoah as a symbolic political gesture, indicating that the valley was now open for settling from the east. Upon his return, he gave each member of his expedition a small golden horseshoe. Thus was the Order of the Golden Horseshoe born, a wonderful legend, full of pomp and chivalry. It certainly beat any exploration story the existing mountain folk had. So, in time, it became common to attribute opening the wilderness to Spotswood, not Lederer.

For generations afterward, the common folk of the mountains took their lumps from the Anglophile civilization that dominated Virginia society. The mountain Germans became known as the "dumb Dutch" or the "slop bucket Dutch." Their language was ridiculed as "a crumbling patois."

The Scotch-Irish mountaineers fared little better. Carl Bridenbaugh describes them as "undisciplined, emotional, courageous, aggressive, pugnacious, fiercely intolerant and hard-drinking, with a tendency to indolence, they nevertheless produced ambitious leaders with the virtues of the warrior and politican. . . . As viewed by others these were hard and unlovely qualities, effective in the new country withal."

An outstanding example of the unyielding, proud mountain spirit is Jost Hite of Winchester. Hite sailed to Virginia from Alsace in his own schooner and migrated into the mountains during early colonial times. He built himself a log cabin as a temporary home, then set about building the first stone house in the Shenandoah Valley.

Hite had received a 100,000-acre land grant from Virginia Governor Gooch, but when court challenges stripped the German of his title, Hite refused to go. Lord Fairfax himself ordered the intransigent immigrant to get out. Hite stayed put. He planted, plowed and prayed. He lived his life in the fashion he wished, following the customs of his culture.

Jost Hite died on his own Virginia land and was buried there. He refused to yield the freedom he'd come here to find. Mountain folk, like Hite, grew tough.

As an old Valley folk song says:

> They raised them rough, they raised them well,
> When their feet were set in the paths of hell
> They put in their souls the fear of God
> And tanned their hides with a stiff ram-rod.

Not just the mountain men, but their women, too, were tough. The sad legend behind the name of Hungry Mother State Park, for example, tells of the grit of Molly Marley. Kidnapped by the Indians, Molly and her little son managed to escape and flee into the woods. After days of living off nothing but wild berries, Molly grew weak and died near the base of what is now Molly's Knob. But she had gotten close enough to a village for her child to crawl to safety. Reportedly the boy's first words to his rescuers were: "Hungry—Mother."

The mountain folk in their stoic fashion have weathered the

buffeting they've received over the years as best they could. Shortly after the Civil War, an Augusta newspaper wrote implacably that: "The hardy Scotch-Irish above us are used to persecution, and the Dutch below are constitutionally phlegmatic, and the soil of the Valley is generous still."

Today, at least in part because of assimilation forced by belittlement, the mountain character has submerged into the larger Virginia character. But isolated pockets of the old style still remain. In locales such as Criders, near Brocks Gap in Rockingham County or Jerome and Orkney Grade in Shenandoah Valley, Dutch is sometimes spoken still.

And a few German customs still hang on. An example is the Christmastime tradition of "bellsniggling." The name comes from the German word *Belshnickle,* which means Santa Claus. About a week before Christmas, men and women trade clothes and hide behind homemade masks. Then they go about from house to house, and the householder is supposed to try and guess who is who.

Poverty follows the mountain people like a chill wind through their green glades. A short summer can ruin their crops. And a depression in the coal business, which happens rather often, can bring their economy to a dead halt.

During the recurring economic dry spells, mountain families are forced to move away. They head down to Richmond or even farther afield looking for work. As a result, the population of the mountains has steadily declined in recent decades.

But even when mountain people have left the hills physically, they haven't really left in their hearts. Many still vote in their old districts by mail. Almost universally, they express the desire to head back home when times get better. And, noted a local philosopher, "they all come home to die."

In the quiet, green-swept hollows of their homeland—and carried with them through all their trails and roaming—the mountain people treasure two things: their music and their religion.

The music is a blend of bluegrass and balladry. It has a pounding beat and the sharp fast picking of country dance music, but always an overtone of the sadness of mountain life. If the tune is perky and upbeat, the lyrics may tell a story of loneliness or pain. As the banjos rip and the guitars hum, the singer, in the nasal intonation of mountains performance, sings:

She walked through the corn
Leading down to the river
Her hair shown like gold
In the hot morning sun.
She took all the love
That this poor boy could give her,
And left me to die
Like a fox on the run.

Everybody knows
The reason for the fall
When woman tempted man
Down in paradise's hall.
This woman tempted me, all right,
And took me for a ride
But like the lonely fox
I need a place to hide.

Come take a glass of wine
And fortify your soul,
We'll talk about the world
And friends we used to know.
I'll illustrate a girl
Who put me on the floor.
The game is nearly up,
And the hounds are at the door.

For the mountain people, music is more than entertainment. The staccato rhythm of the chords and the stories of overcoming sorrow and strife are an affirmation of their ability to cope with their lives and with their absence from home. More than with any other form of music, mountain songs bring a picture of a particular way of life to mind.

A great celebration of mountain music is the annual festival in Galax where thousands of mountain folk, former mountain folk and curious outsiders take over the town of 6,000 for an orgy of lickin', pickin' and celebration. Instrumentalists put their fingers through incredible efforts to garner the paltry prize money. The important prize, of course, isn't the money, but the acknowledgment of being the best picker around.

The crowds flow over the hillsides, swaying and stomping to a succession of songs that evoke the local lore like an ancient tribe's recitation of the tribal history. To absorb the sounds of Galax is to bathe in the mountain culture.

Mountain religion is simple and uncompromising. Jesus came to earth and died for our sins, believe in him and be saved. Refuse to believe, deviate from his path and be damned. The mountain ministers who preach stern doctrine with a touch of vaudeville are a mix of John Calvin and Billy Sunday.

Most successful among them is Jerry Falwell.

Falwell's career represents an incredible success story; to his followers, it must seem like the workings of divine providence. In 1956 Falwell founded the Thomas Road Baptist Church in Lynchburg with about thirty-five members. He began a radio program and then a local television show six months later. Now, Falwell's church has 18,000 members, employs close to a thousand people, and runs on an annual budget of over $50 million. His old time "Gospel Hour" is beamed to some 320 television and 277 radio stations all over the country. Last year, he carried his message across the nation with "I Love America" rallies, which took him to all fifty states.

"There sitting by your television, God loves you," Falwell tells his audience each Sunday, his baritone voice registering cosy familiarity, "and so bow your heads. Tell Him 'I'm a sinner and pray for me.'" A stocky amiable man in his late forties with a beaming, oval face, Falwell looks a bit like a chubby Karl Malden. His oratorical style is that of a bone-bred preacher, a maestro of the pulpit, who moves effortlessly from ingratiating familiarity to orotund theatricality. "We must all study the Bible . . . and learn to believe in God," he cries out his hands shaping his words. A chorus of amens swells in counterpoint.

Sterner religious traditions are maintained by the mountain Amish and Old Order Mennonite communities. The Mennonites have set up their old-fashioned but highly efficient farms near Kempsville, Gladys and Schuyler. Amish folk live near Stuart's Draft, Mount Zion and Catless, which is just forty miles from Washington.

These industrious, pious, old world people still hold their church services in German, wear the black, modest garb of their forefathers, and follow, to varying degrees, the uncompromising rules of behavior that came over from Germany. Some Amish, though, have given up their horses and buggies for pick-ups and tractors.

However, even with many variations from congregation to congregation, and some modernization, these true believers have, in the words of a review of Virginia's German population, "once again brought to Virginia the simple heritage which the native Virginia German stock lost by its complete integration."

One other tradition that the conservative German sects keep is the age-old manner of singing with shape notes. In olden times, music was reckoned in modes, rather than keys, and a form of musical notation grew up that noted the position of a note in the modal scale by means of shape, rather than position on a staff.

In mountain churches you can still sometimes find a shape-note hymnal in which the finely inked, mysterious looking forms snake across the page like runes. The seven notes of the shape note scale are geometric forms corresponding to the scale

Do, Re, Mi, Fa, Sol, La, Ti.

As recently as the mid-1960s, shape-note music was still being printed by small Mennonite presses in the hills.

Hand in hand with the religion of Virginia's mountain people go their natural dramatic tendencies. They love good stories and good audiences for them. They like to create dramatic situations out of everyday life. The commonest occurrence will become a little playlet upon retelling.

Well, I was a-waitin' for the bus and there was this crow on the fence just fussin' and a-frettin for all it was worth. You know, you could just tell this animal was full a something or other. And then here comes this other crow, sort of sneakin' onto the fence. Well, Lordy have mercy, but that first crow took out after the second one! She sqawked and batted the other one with her wings and chased him up and down the fence, peckin' away at him. And, I'm tellin' you truly, I could feel for that second crow. I knew just what he was a-goin' through. I swear to heaven, I have never seen nothin' look so much like my old woman lightin' out after me when I've been out carousin' in my life. No, sir. That was one henpecked crow.

Also, reflecting this dramatic appreciation and an interesting anomaly in Virginia's mountain culture, is the Barter Theatre, situated way out in Abingdon. In an age when many big cities can't support a full theater season Abingdon and the surrounding hills have managed quite well for years.

During the Depression. Bob Porterfield decided to take a group of indigent actors away from the penniless city, to the country where they could perform in exchange for farm goods and crafts. A barter theater.

The Barter survived right up through the 1940s by accepting bushels of apples, baskets of vegetables, once even a pair of rattlesnakes for admission. The actors lived in an abandoned girl's school, and everyone pitched in to help (including a few well-heeled city friends of Porterfield's who sometimes kicked in money).

Finally, in 1946 the Virginia legislature appropriated a stipend for The Barter (after Porterfield informed the legislators, that his operation represented "late night entertainment you could talk about") and it became Virginia's state theater.

Ernest Borgnine, Gregory Peck and Patricia Neal, among many others, began their acting careers at The Barter, which is still going strong today and still accepting produce in exchange for seats. (They will, however, also—gladly—take cash these days.)

The Barter tends to favor comedy, a natural tendency because mountain audiences treasure a good joke. They love to spin yarns among friends. They love dryly humorous tales that puncture pomposity or big-city views.

One of the most often told tales concerns Daniel Boone, who, of course, began his career in Virginia's hills. Boone left for Tennessee only when he felt the Virginia mountains were getting too crowded. In any case, the story goes that Boone, a venerable figure at age ninety, was asked if he'd ever been lost during his long career. The mountain man thought it over and replied:

"No, I never got lost. But I was *bewildered* once for three full days."

Another tale involves the Rawhide Baptist Church, which found it had some extra money to fool around with. The Deacons met to decide what to do, and one suggested:

"Let's use the money to buy a chandelier."

At that point a brother leaped to his feet and protested, "I object! This 'chandelier' is a strange word that nobody can spell, besides which, if we got one nobody'll be able to play it. And anyway, if we're going to spend money, the first thing we need is more light in here!"

A third story centers on the Civil War battle of Seven Pines. A mountain mother heard that her two boys, Jim and John, were both at the battle. All night long she prayed to God to watch over Jim. Finally, her husband, got irritated. "Why don't you pray for Johnny?" he asked. "Because," the mother replied calmly, "if they's seven pines down there, I know my Johnny's behind one of 'em."

Another famous tale from the hills involves the legendary hunter "Rimfire" Hanrick of Webster Springs. Hanrick one day found himself confronted with thirteen wild turkeys and only one shot left in his long rifle. He pondered the problem and came up with a novel way to bag the lot:

"I noticed the whole thirteen of 'em was perched on a limb no bigger'n a man's wrist. That gives me an idear. Loadin' my bar'l about a quarter way full o' powder and rammin' the last bullet down on hit, I tuk aim at the limb of the tree an' fired. The bullet split the limb and let them there turkeys' toes drop down in the crack. Before they had time to fly off, the split closed up an' ketched their toes. I clumb up the tree, cut off the limb with my pocket knife, and packed the whole dang flock home just as I ketched 'em."

From time to time the unique humor of mountain people has been known to slip over into downright peculiarity. Take the case of Polka Dot Creek Charlie Fields. For reasons he took with him to the grave, Charlie turned his homestead north of Lebanon into a phantasmagoria of polka dots. His shack, out buildings, even a hand-built wooden airplane in the front yard, were covered with wavy lines of vibrantly colored dots. Mountain folk accept such eccentricity with just a shrug of their shoulders, saying, "Well, that was Charlie for you."

To outsiders the mountains are a pleasure land. A place of mountain lakes for summer vacations; of Skyline Drive for magnificent views of millions of leafy acres bursting into color for an autumn extravaganza; of ski resorts with slick slopes and slicker accommodations.

This view of the mountains as being beautiful but worthless may have given rise to a much-told tale about how the striking mountain, Massanutten, got its name:

Once a Shenandoah explorer came upon a slave as he wandered through the mountains.

"Tell me," he asked politely, "do these mountains hold any gold?"

"Massa, no," answered the black man.

"What about coal?"

"Massa, no."

"Well, what is there of value in these God-forsaken hills?"

"Massa, nuttin' "

These days, Massanutten has "somethin"—one of Virginia's finest, most modern ski resorts, a wintertime lure for skiers from as far away as New York.

But the natives see the magnificent views as a thin green or white skin stretched over a black heart of coal. The lifelong struggle to get coal out of the ground is the central fact of much mountain life. And the basic futility of that struggle has engendered a tremendous fatalism in mountain folk.

"I been going down the mines for thirty-four years," an old miner, his face like a wrinkled shirt, says. "Sure it's better now than it were. But all that means is, now I get electric lights in Hell instead of lanterns."

For the miner and his family, the question is not *if* the next tragedy will occur, but *when.* It's not if the man will get some degree of black lung, but how long he'll be able to work before it hits. The life is not pretty and it's not fun.

The mountain people see themselves as being the ones who are courageous or foolish enough to do the dirty work for the rest of society. They see their labor as largely unappreciated. They feel everybody else cares only about the price of coal, not about the price the miners pay to get the coal for them.

This is another reason behind this stand-offishness. *You,* they radiate to outsiders, *don't face our worry, our grief, our trouble. You can't know what we go through, so don't judge us and don't try to know us. Go down the in mine a few times, and then we'll talk.*

The mountain folk save their wit and candor for the places where they are comfortable: the home and the general store. In many mountain communities the general store still plays a central role as meeting place, information exchange and social club. It provides a tie with the outside world that doesn't require contact, like an airlock on a submarine. The combination of sociability and remoteness found in the country stores, prompted Virginia Moore

69

to state: "Norfolk may not **be Virginia. Richmond** may not be Virginia, but the country stores, in desperate need of paint, are the *very* Virginia—isolated, lonely, yet intensely sociable."

The mountain home is the warm place, threadbare though it may be, where virtually everything good that's likely to happen to a mountain person will take place. Homes in these hills are truly seen as refuges.

Such a mountain home nurtured the poetic nature of Willa Cather whose novels, such as *My Antonía,* have elevated the standards of American literature. The Cather family lived at Willowshade Farm, near Gore. In the 1870s, Willa grew up in these "high hills which shut out the sun . . . early." Her grandmother taught her to read and write, and she learned about the land by wandering the hills with the family sheepdog, Vic. When she was nine, Willa's family moved to the Middlewest, but the "tranquil . . . ordered and serene" Virginia spirit imbued in the Shenandoah stayed with her forever.

The best metaphor for life in the mountains probably lies in the style of dancing—clogging. View a clogger from the waist up and he looks like he is gently bobbing his head in time to the music. But from below he is electric. His feet move in a shuffling blur, stomping and sliding along the floor almost too fast for the eye to see. The movement is one of ecstasy, vitality and great strength.

That's what mountain life is like. Quiet, almost placid from one view. Yet, masking passion, courage, temperament and wit, moving to the beat of that stirring mountain music, while the preacher shouts, "Amen!"

Beneath the thin green skin, Virginia's mountains hold a black heart of coal, the hard center of many mountain lives.

The ghostly presence of a miner, his world illuminated only by his headlamp.

Where mountain folk go, they bring their hills with them. This scene was shot in Richmond.

Etta Blackburn isn't going to be worried about any fuel oil shortages this winter. The 78-year-old Grayson County resident cuts firewood, which she says is one of her hobbies. (UPI *mg/Gene Dalton*).

The grim face of a performer at a Virginia mountain amusement park recalls the rugged woodsmen who opened up the region.

Gnarled farmer hands invented, and still play, the music we now call bluegrass.

Picker Keith Sturgiss warms up at the Old Time Fiddler's convention in
Galax.

A group of visitors makes impromptu bumper-to-bumper music in the parking lot at Galax.

Once each year, on July 4, the world-famous Statler Brothers come home to Virginia's hills for a benefit concert.

Virginia's mountains are home to some of the best ski areas in the East.

Snow frosts the square before the Albermarle County Courthouse.

The
Black Spirit

Virginia holds the dubious honor of being the spot where the first blacks were brought ashore in America. The first notation of blacks on this continent can be found in John Rolfe's letter to Sir Edwin Sandys, treasurer of the Virginia Company:

> About the latter end of August, a Dutch man of Warr of the burden of a 160 tunes arrived at Point Comfort, the commanders name Capt. Jope, his pilott for the West Indies, one Mr. Marmaduke an Englishman. . . . He brought not anything but 20 and odd Negroes, which the Governor and Cape Marchant bought for victually (whereof he was in great need as he ptended) at the best and easiest rates they could. . . .

The tobacco economy of the early South needed labor. There weren't enough white bodies to go around. The settlers had tried Indians, but they had proved incorrigible. So, the availability of Negro workers proved quite a boon to the emerging community.

A few souls raised the question about whether treatment of blacks as property was a just and Christian idea, but they were drowned by a chorus of profiteers, allowing the institution of slavery to spread from Virginia throughout the South.

It must be admitted, though, that while Virginia used slavery and profited from it, the state never seems to have been fully comfortable with the institution. This discomfort didn't prevent the state's slave population from leaping from 300 in 1650 to 540,000 in 1850, but it has provided some comfort for white Virginians who have had trouble reconciling slavery with the image of their fair-minded, humanistic ancestors.

George Bagby, for one, blamed the continuation of slavery in Virginia on outside forces. He compared the situation to a cuff button:

"This button here upon my cuff is valueless, whether for use or ornament, but you shall not tear it from me and spit in my face besides; no, not if it cost me my life. And if your time passed in an attempt so to take it, then my time and my every thought shall be spent in preventing such an outrage. Left alone the Virginian would gladly have made an end to slavery, but . . . malevolance and meddling bound it up with every interest that was dear to his heart—wife, home, honor . . ."

While the storm clouds of war gathered, Virginia went through painful contortions trying to figure out what to do. Many leaders were weak on the issue of slavery and weaker still on the notion of secession; Virginia, after all, was the heart of America up to that point. To many of that age, Virginia couldn't be separated from America, she was America.

As Marshall Fishwick notes in his excellent history, *Virginia: A New Look at the Old Dominion:* "For many Virginians, the dilemma was moral rather than political. For years the state's leaders had questioned the validity of slavery and nullification. What they were willing to defend were freedom, justice and—most of all—honor.

E. A. Pollard put it this way: "The glory of history is indifferent to events—it is simply honor. The name of Virginia in this war is historically and absolutely more important to us than any other element of the contest."

And Mary Boykin Chestnut, in her fascinating *Diary from Dixie,* noted at the time of the Confederate government's formation: "They say Virginia has no grievance. She comes out on a point of honor."

At one point a state convention voted *not* to secede. Then President Lincoln called for 75,000 soldiers to put down the rebellion begun with the firing on Ft. Sumter. Virginia's Governor Lechter would send not a man. On April 17, 1861, the Virginia Convention voted reluctantly to break up the Union their forefathers had invented.

Virginia's large black population has grown from these cruel roots into a potent force in state affairs. Black contribution to Virginian culture has been extensive, in spite of the state's paternalistic racism. As one local pundit put it, even when they were disenfranchised, Virginia's blacks thought of themselves as Virginians first. That's one reason why Virginia's cities were spared much of the racial violence that plagued most of the country during the 1960s. To riot would be very un-Virginian.

In the past twenty years Virginia's blacks have made enormous strides toward fulfilling their role as movers and shakers in their home state, sometimes with the help of Virginia's whites, often in spite of them. And but anchored to the twin supports of church and family, Virginia's blacks have 200 years practice at overcoming obstacles quietly, patiently and with dignity.

Take the story of James Martin, for example: "I was born in Virginia in 1847. My mother was a slave, and my grandfather was one of the early settlers in Virginia. He was born in Jamaica, and his master took him to England. When the English came to Virginia, they brought us along as servants, but when they got here, everybody had slaves, so we was slaves, too. My mother was born in the West Indies.

"A man named Martin brought my grandfather here, and took his name. And when Master was ready to die, he made a will, and it said the youngest child in the slaves must be made free, so that was my father, and he was made free when he was sixteen. That left me and my brothers and sisters all free, but all the rest of the family was slaves.

"My mother was a slave near Alexandria. The master's daughter, Miss Liza, read to my mother, so she got some learning. When my mother's owner died, he left her to Miss Liza, and then my father met my mother and told her they should get married. My mother said to Miss Liza: 'I'd like fine to marry Preston Martin.' Miss Liza says, 'You can't do that, 'cause he's a free nigger and your children would be free You gotta marry one of the slaves.' Then Miss Liza lines up ten or fifteen of the slave men for my mother to pick from, but Mother says she don't like any of 'em, she wants to marry Preston Martin. Miss Liza argues, but my mother is just stubborn, so Miss Liza says, 'I'll talk to the master.' He says, 'I can't lose property like that, and if you can raise $1,200 you can buy yourself free.' So my mother and my father saves money, and it takes a long time, but one day they goes to the master and lays down the money, and they gits married. Master don't like it, but he's promised and he can't back out."

Today, blacks have begun to make themselves felt as a political force in the state. Richmond's mayor is black, as is its school superintendent. In Surry County, the reins of local government were recently wrested away from staid hands by a black coalition.

And, in both urban and rural areas, there are strong church- and family-centered black communities. Virginia's blacks are mainly working people. They build the ships in Newport News, roll the cigarettes in Richmond, mine coal in Newton and harvest tobacco in Southside. Their communities are solid and middle class for the most part.

Virginia is still no mecca of racial harmony and fairness, but it is a healthier environment for blacks than most Northern cities.

The role of blacks in Virginia affairs, of course, began with slavery. But early Virginia blacks did far more than pick tobacco and serve their owners. Numerous black soldiers were honored for bravery by the Virginia Legislature after the Revolutionary War. That old Confederate Robert E. Lee himself expressed the opinion that blacks made excellent soldiers.

And, while Virginia's black have been more polite in their struggle than their compatriots elsewhere, they have been far from quiescent, even at times flaring with historic rage.

Margaret Douglas of Norfolk, for instance, intimated the coming of passive resistance through her stubborn refusal to stop teaching free black children to read in the 1850s. Her four-room school was the first educational facility for free blacks in America and was in flat defiance of laws that banned "the instruction of all colored persons by means of books or printed papers." Tried for her "crime," Douglas wrote: "I am happy to say, although I was afterwards cruelly cast into prison and otherwise unjustly dealt with, I have the satisfaction of knowing that I suffered in a good and righteous cause . . . I shall be only a single sufferer under the operation of one of the most inhuman and unjust laws that ever disgraced the state book of a civilized community."

More strident and epochal was the protest of the slave Nat Turner. Turner was born in Southampton County October 2, 1800, the slave of a small, but well-to-do plantation owner. An intense young boy, he absorbed from his African mother an abiding hatred for bondage. He soaked up reading from one of his master's sons and religion from the slave community.

Religion made a tremendous impact on Turner. He had been born with peculiar makings, which he came to believe were marks of destiny from the Lord. During the 1820s, Turner became almost obsessed with religious devotion. He began to see himself as God's chosen messenger to the slaves; a Black Moses come to lead his people to freedom.

Educated and physically striking, Turner became a natural leader among slaves. His magnetic personality and deeply felt convictions drew their attention and riled them up.

In 1831, after being sold to a craftsman named Travis, Turner saw an eclipse of the sun. He saw this as a sign from God that the time to throw off the slave masters was at hand. He devised a plan for capturing the armory at Jerusalem, Virginia, the county seat. Then he and his army of followers would eluded pursuit by striking for the Great Dismal Swamp, thirty miles away.

On August 21, Turner and seven trusted companions exploded in a feverish campaign of revenge. Travis and his family were murdered in their beds. Then the band set out for Jerusalem. Over the next two days fifty-one white people were slain. Turner's band grew to seventy-five unruly followers.

But the combined firepower of aroused local whites and a 3,000-man state militia unit crushed the revolt. The whites, in fear and retaliation, murdered revolutionaries and peaceful slaves alike for six weeks, while they combed the countryside for Turner.

The rebel slave was hanged, but his bold insurrection set off harsh repressions against slaves that probably helped harden attitudes in the North and brought on the Civil War. And, in the hearts of slaves everywhere who heard the story of his exploit, he awoke pride, rage and hope. Throughout the war slaves spoke of Jerusalem only partly in religious tribute. Covertly, they were paying homage to the sacrifice of Nat Turner.

Even earlier than Nat Turner, the slave Gabriel led an insurrection that might just have taken Richmond if the weather had been right. Gabriel, a giant fellow who was owned by Thomas Prosser of Henrico, had enlisted some thousand slaves from the area to throw off their chains and take over Richmond. The story of how the insurrection didn't happen brings to mind unsettling thoughts of what might have been.

On August 30, 1800, so reports go, two slaves owned by Mosby Sheppard, told him that an insurrection had been planned for that night. The slave Gabriel, they told their owner, would lead a horde of blacks to the city, killing the whites and taking over.

Sheppard alerted authorities, and Governor James Monroe called out the militia and sealed the city off. The sentries patrolling the roads outside of town reported eerily that instead of following normal practice and heading toward town on a hot Saturday night, all the blacks they saw were heading into the countryside.

Late that afternoon a huge thunderstorm turned the country roads to muck and made streams impassable. This happenstance of weather apparently is all that kept the slaves from gathering in the woods, collecting their makeshift weapons and marching on the town.

After the flashpoint passed, hundreds of blacks were rounded up and questioned. Fifty conspirators were arrested. Gabriel himself fled to Norfolk, but was captured on ship and returned to Richmond. Forty slaves were executed for the plot.

It is ironic that Virginians noted for their ceaseless pursuit of liberty should have had so hard a time understanding the quest for liberty in others. But they did, and blacks suffered for it. As David Mays put it "Gabriel had dared to fight for freedom with the very words of 'death or liberty' consciously or otherwise reversing the cry of Patrick Henry. But Henry's oratory was not meant for slaves."

In an embryonic way, the revolts by Gabriel and Nat Turner presaged the feelings of black rage and black power that would impel the violent demands of the 1960s. They said early on that a white establishment would only react to a force great enough to cause fear.

In the years since the reunion of the states, Virginia race relations have had their ups and downs. Reconstruction hit Virginia less hard than many other places, so the residual level of bitterness between the races was not as high. But the taints of segregationism didn't leave Virginia untouched, and the battles over state school integration in this century were surely Virginia's worst public performance in history. The U. S. Supreme Court, in the landmark Brown vs. Board of Education case, had ruled that separate-but-equal schools, such as Virginia had employed, were inherently segregationist, even if all facilities were made identical. Therefore, Virginia schools would have to integrate, whether they liked it or not.

They didn't like it. After a flurry of conciliatory statements, Virginia's leaders scurried behind the segregationist banner of Senator Harry F. Byrd. Black leaders were consulted by the state, only to see if they would be willing to accept continued segregation. They would not.

Virginia's leaders began a death dance with the inevitable adoption of full integration. The doctrine of massive resistance emerged from this quadrille, a call to stop federal meddling in state affairs, to never give up and accept forced integration.

When the school year rolled round, the crunch came. Faced with the prospect of integrating or staying closed, public schools in many Virginia communities stayed closed. Most reopened after maneuvering in the state house and an impassioned plea from Governor Lindsay Almond. But in Prince Edward County, where the Brown case began, officials kept the schools closed for four years. White children went to private schools and blacks stayed home.

Finally, in 1963 Governor Albertis Harrison, created a plan to open publicly funded schools for Prince Edward County blacks and forced the local schools back open.

The massive resistance period was certainly the nadir in Virginia's racial relations. It was the only time in decades that sheer animosity guided public decisions on either side. But it represented an irreparable break with the past. It was the necessary catharsis that shook Virginia into the modern age of racial equality.

As Louis Rubin says in his history of Virginia: "To the Virginians of Harry Byrd's generation the threat of such overwhelming chance was so ominous that they had been led into massive resistance against it. So intense was their affection for Virginia, in the political and social forms that they had been accustomed to think of it, that they could not conceive of its continuing to be Virginia in terms other than those they knew."

But the very forms they wished to preserve carried Virginia through the crisis. And the essential qualities of the state, built up by its black citizens as well as its white, survived admirably, probably even enhanced by the removal of rancor and the residual bitterness of years of disaffection.

Over the years, Virginia has produced numerous black leaders. John Mercer Langston was the only Virginia black ever elected to Congress. The son of a white planter and a slave he achieved posts as Minister to Haiti, first president of the Virginia Normal and Collegiate Institute (now Virginia State) and Dean of Howard University Law School, as well as serving a term in Washington.

John Jaspar was a preacher in Richmond whose stirring sermons made him famous all over the country. His congregation was located on an island in the James River. It was Jaspar, in one of his best-known sermons, who uttered one of the most famous quotes of any Virginian black or white. "There are four races of men," he thundered, "Huguenots, Abyssinians, Hottentots and Virginians. And Virginians are the only race that doesn't have to be born again!"

But the most influential of all was Booker T. Washington.

Washington was born in a dingy one-room hovel. The floor was dirt. There were no windows. It was, to say the least, an inauspicious start.

At age nine, Washington moved with his newly emancipated family to Malden, West Virginia. Three years later he began school. He would work five hours in the mines or furnaces before school each day and would return to work after class. It was at school that Booker found his last name. When asked by his teacher who he was, the young man, who had known only a first name throughout his boyhood, dubbed himself Washington figuring that would make him "equal to the situation."

One day at the mines, Washington overheard two men talking about a school for blacks in Virginia, called the Hampton Institute. Determined to take advantage of it, he walked the five hundred miles to Richmond.

Washington grew into a fiercely intellectual as well as an exceedingly fair and patient man. In typical Virginia fashion he counseled progress and change in moderation. His ability to deal diplomatically with whites led to his appointment as an advisor to Presidents Roosevelt and Taft. This conciliatory stance has caused him to be labeled, unfairly, as an Uncle Tom in recent years. But, behind the scenes he pushed hard for better treatment of blacks.

"Whatever one thinks of the hypocrisy involved in talking one way in public on a pressing issue and another quite different way in private," wrote Virginius Dabney, "the fact remains that Washington would have been in a hopeless position if, in the 1890s or early 1900s he had openly launched a drive for complete citizenship rights and full equality for the Negro. Public opinion in all parts of the United States was far from ready for such doctrine. So Washington followed policies acceptable to his day and became one of the most influential Virginians in history."

Washington preached a brand of pragmatism not too far removed from today's Jesse Jackson. Blacks, he said, must drink the water from where they stand, rather than die of thirst waiting for better water ahead. They should strive for stability in their lives and excellence in their work as it was available to them, instead of holding out for unattainable lives and jobs. Like Jackson, he asked blacks to be the best they could be under the circumstances.

The most popular black Virginian was Bill Robinson, who achieved fame and fortune as a toe-tapping Mr. Bojangles in Hollywood movies of the 1930s. Robinson stands as a symbol both of the achievements and limitations of blacks up to the present day. A man of enormous charm and talent, he reached the highest levels of show business and became a figure squarely set in the pantheon of American performing legends. And yet he was limited by his race to roles as the smiling darkie sidekick of the cute little white star.

Everything he performed was tailor-made for his white partners. Heaven only knows how much greater a performer Bojangles could have been if he could have portrayed anything beyond a grinning stereotype.

One of the most amazing black women in history, Maggie L. Walker, rose from life in a Richmond kitchen slave's house, to become the first black female bank president in America. She did this in 1903.

Through grit and determination Maggie Walker managed to get herself educated in nineteenth-century Richmond. She got a job teaching other blacks, but left it—an unheard of thing for a black woman—to study business. In 1889 she became executive secretary-treasurer for the fraternal Order of St. Luke, a black insurance society. She had thirty dollars in her treasury and made all of eight dollars a month.

By 1924 the Order had 100,000 members and fifty-five full-time employees. And by the end of Maggie Walker's life in 1934 it was a multi-million dollar operation with seven hundred branches in twenty-eight states.

After leaving St. Luke's she continued working with her bank as board chairman. Over the years the St. Luke's Penny Savings Bank which she founded grew and merged, until today it is the Consolidated Bank and Trust Company, one of the largest black-held financial institutions in the country.

Outside of business, Maggie Walker poured energy and ingenuity into civic projects that benefited blacks. Although confined to a wheelchair the last twenty years of her life, she formed a home for indigent Negro girls, established Richmond's community center and supported untold other causes in her busy life. Her death was mourned as much by the white establishment as by the black community she had struggled for.

Stereotypes don't have nearly as strong a hold for blacks in Virginia today. Blacks can be seen everywhere in the state, doing everything all Virginians do, at all social levels. Portraits of two black Richmonders show the diversity of black attitude in modern Virginia.

Sa'ad El Amin is a firebrand. This Black Muslim lawyer wants to stir up things. He is feisty, a showboater given to publicity stunts and sharply worded denunciations of any who get in the way of his goals. He is the self-styled champion of the little man, the hotshot lawyer who will take on the small man's case and make a pretty penny for himself, too. His advertisements embarrass the legal establishment but draw customers. His blasts at the black mayor of Richmond cause chagrin in the local black-power structure. Many dislike Amin intensely; others respect him for his refusal to knuckle under to anybody and for his unabashed determination to be utterly himself at all times at all costs.

Thomas Cannon, on the other hand, is the personification of gentle generosity. This black Richmond postman gives away a large portion of his income every year. To strangers. Without strings or fanfare. Cannon believes that all humans are brothers and sisters in the fullest sense of the words. When he reads or hears about another human being in need of a hand, Cannon sends a $1,000 check. A gift from brother to brother. Sometimes the gift helps pay off a pressing debt. Other times it is symbolic, such as when Cannon sent a check to the widow of a policeman slain by a black man. "I wanted to let her know that all blacks were not bad," he said. Cannon lives in genteel poverty in a small house on Richmond's Church Hill. In his front room hangs a display of coins blown up to huge proportions, to remind Cannon "that money is only a symbol. It doesn't mean anything. Only the way you act with your fellow man means anything."

Education has always played a larger role in the lives of Vir-

94

ginia's blacks than is typical of other southern states, or in fact of the rest of the country. Hampton Institute has been educating Virginia blacks since 1868. And Virginia Union University, founded in 1865, has grown from its original home in what had been Lumpkins Jail— a lockup for incorrigibles who had fought being sold into slavery— to an extensive modern campus today. In the original school building, cells had become classrooms and whipping blocks had become lecterns. Today, Virginia Union's striking African tower is a Richmond landmark.

The words of a character in *The Book of Numbers,* a novel by Richmond-born black author Robert Dean Pharr, convey black Virginia's antipathy for ignorance:

> Never ask me to condone the Negro's ignorance. I will do all in my power to eradicate it, but please do not ask me to forgive it. And besides, ignorance needs no champions. It is a powerful thing that can crush truth to the ground without a whisper.

To move from whispering to shouting, let's now look at the steadiest element in Virginia black culture over the years—religion. If the general store is the center of a Virginia mountain town, the church is the heart of every black community. It's the house of prayer, the meeting hall, the social club and the gossip center.

It's a loud, soulful, happy, stirring place to be. You can hear the service in a black church while standing on the street. The faith is unrestrained. The testimony fervent and loudly declaimed. The singing is so rich and rambunctious, sitting still is out of the question.

In some cases, today, the black church is taking itself to the white world. Larry Bland's All Volunteer choir from the Second Baptist Church in Richmond, for instance, has taken its unrestrained Gospel-raising, duck-your-head-'cause-here-comes-the-Lord music to white audiences all over. Even in blasé New York cafes, the choir has stirred up white crowds and gotten them out of their seats roaring with praise.

If black church services are stirring, a black baptism at the ocean's edge is stunning. A crowd, all in white, fills the beach in all directions. The minister, his Bible held aloft, strides into the surf bellowing the words of John the Baptist and the Prophets. The crowd sings and shouts, claps and sways. The surf pounds against the beach. The stiff ocean wind swirls skirts and billows jackets. Arms outstretched against the wind, the minister calls for a sister to be baptized. She joins him in the water.

"Oh Lord, accept our sister . . ."

She goes down, comes up, goes down. The crowd on the beach shouts with delight.

"Amen! Good for you sister. Oh, sweet Jesus . . ."

And the sun shines down on upraised shining, joyous, black faces.

Even a supposedly neutral observer gets so caught up in the event it takes an effort of will to keep from plowing into the waves with everyone else and proclaiming your soul for Jesus.

Forty-five years ago, the Virginia Writer's Project pointed toward today's era of promise for black Virginians after generations of patience and struggle:

> To Virginia's shores the first black man was brought and enslaved; on Virginia soil his freedom finally was assured. By the sweat of his brow the Virginia Negro has paid for that freedom. This is his home, for the strength of his muscles has gone into its building. The cleared forests, the rolling farmlands, the bridged rivers, the thriving cities and towns, the stately mansions are mute testimony to his labors. Work has been his heritage, and his hope is that they may come some day into a fair share of the fruits of his labors.

By and large, Virginia's blacks are approaching their fair share. They are being accepted as full partners in the running of the state they helped to create.

Blacks in Virginia today face a promising future. They have begun to make their mark in all facets of state life. Virginia has a real opportunity to become America's showplace of racial cooperation and mutual respect.

"Race relations in the Commonwealth have been transformed," wrote Virginius Dabney, "and many of the manifest injustices from which black citizens suffered have been ended."

This is one ending that is truly a beginning.

Virginia Union University was one of the first institutions of higher education for blacks in the South.

The eyes of age, in the powerful face of a black farm woman.

Muff Jones, 108, the oldest man in Virginia.

State Senator Douglas Wilder, a black power in Virginia government.

Thomas Cannon, the postman philanthropist, gives money to fellow humans in need.

Like a hard-nosed Leprechaun, this coal miner's face is a blend of hard work and gaity.

The cool gaze of a tank operator at Quantico holds professional malice for the enemy.

There is pride in Virginia black communities. Here an old house is spruced up in Roanoke.

The family of Dr. and Mrs. Dennis Warner displays the growing affluence of Virginia's expanding black middle class.

The Military

Virginia trains the soldiers. Virginia builds the ships. She tests the new technologies of war. She houses the strange building where the plans are made. She sends the soldiers overseas and welcomes them back.

And Virginia takes to her breast the many, many dead. "The soil of Virginia," wrote Virginia Moore, "is drenched with blood. No wonder it is red."

From Arlington National Cemetery to the Norfolk Naval Base, Virginia is a soldier state. It has more military installations than any other area. Quite literally, when America goes to war, Virginia goes to war.

The incomparable Walt Whitman expressed most dramatically the dark but dutiful Virginia devotion to military honor:

> Not the long mad ride round the Union lines
> But the smell of the swamp at Seven Pines.
> And Lee in the Dusk before Malvern Hill
> Riding along with his shoulders straight
> Like a sending out of the Scaean Gate.
> The cold intaglio war,
> This is Virginia's Iliad.

Throughout her history Virginia has been militarily important, both as a battleground and as the source for military leaders and soldiers. The state has suffered in every American war. The leaders of the Revolutionary and Confederate Armies were Virginian. Williamsburg fostered the Revolution. And, from Richmond, the Civil War was waged, with the Army of Virginia as the backbone of the Confederate force.

At war's end, President Lincoln's first thought was to see the place where his adversaries had held counsel. "It seems to me that I have been dreaming in a horrid dream for four years," he said, "and now the nightmare is gone. I want to see Richmond."

Since then Virginia has worked hard for war and defense with, not against, the Federal Government.

The military presence in Virginia today has reached the point where soldiering is the state's second largest employer. Military installations cover some 450 square miles of Old Dominion territory.

And military operations contribute some $2,500,000 to Virginia's economy.

All across Virginia one can find intimations of the military. Not only the existing military facilities which are scattered in all corners of the commonwealth, but the reminders of past campaigns and soldiers, as well. At any moment one of Virginia's hundreds of historical markers might inform you that you are walking along the route of Lee's retreat or Washington's advance, that you stand at the spot where Confederate soldiers made a valiant stand or Union raiders struck a bold stroke. You might even, while strolling down a country lane, kick up bits of old cannonballs or grapeshot, colonial army belt buckles or Civil War rifles. In this sense, at least, Virginia's military past has literally sunk into her soil.

Then there are the major military historical sites. Manassas, where Stonewall Jackson got his nickname and the Yankees took their first whipping. Richmond, which fell to the Union forces in confusion and flame. King's Mountain, where stubborn, feisty mountain men slapped the British with a defeat that would lead to the end of the Revolutionary War. Virtually every town in Virginia has some sort of war memorial, and they aren't the result of empty sentimentality, either. Virginia has seen more war than any other site in America. Having been more touched by the violence of conflict, Virginians feel a greater need to remember the sufferings of the past so that they might be avoided in the future. And it is fitting that the state which has seen so much war also houses America's two most important locations of peace—Yorktown and Appomattox.

Had Virginia not played such crucial roles in these wars and in ending them, she might not have seen the nobler side of war and be what she is today. But the Old Dominion has experienced both the agony of war and its fruition and so has a fuller perspective on the experience than other American states.

Of all the places in Virginia where war has touched, none has seen the concentrated warfare that befell Fredricksburg during the Civil War. Four major battles of the Civil War—Fredricksburg, Chancellorsville, Wilderness and Spotsylvania—occurred in the heart of Virginia's Piedmont.

On December 13, 1862, Fredricksburg saw a vicious confrontation between the South's General Robert E. Lee and Union General Ambrose Burnside. Burnside was attempting to slice down along the Potomac toward Richmond. Lee was determined to stop him. Almost 250,000 soldiers crashed together in the fray, with the Confederates hanging on to beat back the Union assault. Some 18,-000 soldiers died.

The Battle of Chancellorsville followed in May of 1863. Burnside's successor, General Joseph Hooker, tried to surprise Lee by splitting his troops. Hooker left a veneer of troops at the line in Fredericksburg, and took the rest of his soldiers upstream, where he crossed in an attempt to sneak around Lee's flank. But Lee surmised the ploy and split his own force, taking the majority of his men west to meet Hooker. The forces collided at Chancellorsville, an estate ten miles from Fredericksburg. Surprised to find the Confederates facing him, Hooker went into a defensive posture. But on May 2 Lee pulled the masterstroke by dividing his troops again, sending a force under General Jackson to sneak through the woods and attack Hooker's flank. The ruse succeeded, but after dark fell, Jackson's own soldiers shot him by mistake, thinking he was a Union spy.

The next day, the Confederates drove into Hooker with a pincer movement which eventually drove him back across the river. Lost in this battle were 30,000 men, including the irreplaceable Jackson.

The later battles were not as decisive in the course of the war, but brought their own significant measure of destruction. The suffering endured by Virginians at Fredericksburg so impressed the famous Civil War correspondent Viztelly, that he wrote of them: "I am lost in admiration at its [the army of Northern Virginia] splendid patriotism, at its wonderful endurance, at its utter disregard for hardships . . ."

But, for all the heroism displayed there, a deep melancholy attached itself to battlefields like Fredericksburg. So much energy was spent there, so much lost, that a person in the proper frame of mind on a warm summer evening, can still feel the sadness of the long-gone soldiers as they rested after wearying days of battle:

> All quiet along the Potomac tonight
> No sound save the rush of the river
> While soft falls the dew on the face of the dead—
> The picket off duty forever.

This intimate relationship with battle and war has given Virginia a special tie with soldiers and the military of today. Perhaps from this springs a fierce insistence on protecting Mother Virginia. And typical is the comment of a backward Civil War private in Ellen Glasgow's novel *The Battleground*. He muses in his simple fashion about his motivations:

> I didn't see how I was goin' to fire my musket, till all of a jiffy a thought jest jumped into my head and sent me bangin' down that hill. "Them folks have set thar feet on ole Virginny," was what I thought. "They've set their feet on ole Virginny, and they've got to take 'em off damn quick!"

The bitterness that welled up in Virginians after the Civil War about the trampling of their beloved state by Yankee soldiers might have had a lot to do with regional tensions up to this day. No one who would invade, burn and conquer Virginia could possibly be worthy of respect, even if he won.

The level of feeling this violation stirred is best expressed in a song written by Inness Randolph, a major in Jeb Stuart's cavalry and a Virginian, that swept the South following the war:

> Three hundred thousand Yankees
> Is stiff in Southern dust;
> We got three hundred thousand
> Before they conquered us;
> They died of Southern fever,
> And Southern steel and shot,
> I wish it was three million
> Instead of what we got!
>
> I can't take up my musket
> And fight 'em now no more;
> But I ain't a-goin' to love 'em,
> Now that is certain sure.
> And I don't want a pardon
> For what I was and am;
> I won't be reconstructed,
> And I don't give a damn.

Today, the living embodiment of Virginia's military tradition is Virginia Military Institute (VMI) in Lexington. At VMI the proud cadets still doff their hats to the campus' statues of Lee and Stonewall Jackson. They are not recalcitrant juvenile delinquents sent off for softening, but the cream of Virginia's youth, proud young men fulfilling a tradition of education and service that sometimes dates back generations in their families.

Before the Civil War made him a hero, Stonewall Jackson taught physics at VMI. He was but a major then, and the cadets mischieviously dubbed him "Old Tom Fool." Professor Jackson was a stickler for discipline and he taught by example. Once, an oft'-told tale relates, Jackson was putting cadets through their paces when a violent storm broke over them. The students dashed for shelter without Jackson's order. But, as an example to them of proper behavior, the major stood at attention in the downpour until drill period was over.

When the War came, it brushed the lives of VMI cadets. As Union troops swept toward Winchester, 257 cadets joined Confederate General John Breckinridge's brigades in a stand at New Market. The young fighters scrambled across the battlefield, successfully taking a Yankee position. Ten of them died and forty-seven were wounded. Their heroism is noted today at VMI's Hall of Valor.

VMI has produced many great soldiers. Matthew Fontaine Maury, a VMI professor, devised wind and current charts of the North Atlantic that revolutionized navigation and still set the standard for Naval charts today. General George S. Patton, too, spent some time at VMI. But the most illustrious graduate of the academy is certainly General George C. Marshall, Army Chief of Staff during World War II and President Truman's Secretary of State. A native Pennsylvanian, Marshall came to his military vocation after a weak start at VMI. Throughout his career, he referred to his VMI years as crucial to his later views and successes. Today, Marshall's Nobel Peace Prize, which he received for devising the Marshall Plan for resurrecting Europe after World War II, stands in a place of honor on campus.

Men don't hold an exclusive franchise on military tradition in Virginia. Women of grit and courage hold important positions in the state's legacy of war.

Clara Barton, the legendary Civil War nurse, performed her exhaustive ministrations at the Battle of Fredericksburg. She converted a manor house on the east shore of the Rappahannock River into a field hospital where she treated many of the horde of wounded Confederate soldiers. Then, she crossed the pontoon bridges laid down by Union General Burnside to serve the Yankee victims. As she crossed, she wrote later, "the water hissing with shot on either side . . . an officer stepped to my side to assist me over the debris at the end of the bridge. While our hands were raised in the act of stepping down, a piece of an exploded shell hissed through us, just below our arms, carrying away a portion of both the skirts of his coat and my dress, rolling along the ground a few rods from us like a harmless pebble in the water."

In Tazewell, each July, the riding club reenacts one of the most valiant and little known heroic acts of the Civil War—the ride of Molly Tynes. She was a young college graduate summering in Tazewell in 1863, when she heard that the 1,000 Union cavalry camped near town were planning to raid Wytheville and wipe it out.

Tynes, grabbed her horse, Fashion, and galloped across the treacherous hills warning the people along the way of the Yankee approach. Aroused, the mountain folk drove the soldiers back and saved the town and its railroad.

A better known, but no less stirring, service in the Confederate War effort was the battlefield charge of Belle Boyd. Belle Boyd was a spy. In May of 1862 she listened through a knot hole in the floor of a closet in the Front Royal Hotel and heard the detailed plans of Yankee officers for the Battle of Front Royal. Boyd raced back to her cottage, wrote down everything she had heard and charged toward the battlefield to give the vital information to Stonewall Jackson. Blithely ignoring the fact that her white sunbonnet, dark blue dress and decorated apron made her stand out like a sore thumb, she ran across the open battlefield as Union bullets whizzed by her head and burned through her skirts.

Exhausted, Boyd passed her note to the open mouthed Jackson and collapsed. Using the information she had provided, the General formulated a classically effective attack. Later, he wrote Boyd that she had provided "immense service to the country."

Virginia's military heritage is reflected in the most extensive array of bases and headquarters of any American state. Virginia has been called the back yard for Washington's military establishment, and the brass have festooned the commonwealth with weapons and soldiers.

Newport News Shipbuilding, the state's biggest private employer, crafts the gigantic floating cities that comprise today's Navy. Thousands of Virginians scurry about the huge hulls of nuclear aircraft carriers, destroyers, escort vessels and supply ships like so many Lilliputians.

The influence of the shipyards spreads up and down the Tidewater triangle, giving the area an atmosphere like the big steel towns up North. Here tough men and women do tough work. They mold strong, simple elements into a sophisticated enormity. They live boom-and-bust existences. When the ships need to be built they work until they want to drop and make good money. But when the ship orders run dry, they are laid off and have to suck in their bellies until times improve.

When the ships are finished, they float downriver toward Norfolk, a cocky sailor town that anchors Virginia's largest population concentration. Norfolk isn't pretty. It's sturdy. You get the impression that if Norfolk rolled up its sleeves you'd see a lot of muscle and a few tattoos. There is a sandy, sea-weathered look to the place; the buildings look old but muscular.

The naval influence on Norfolk can be seen in the more than sixty-four separate naval activities located within fifty miles of town. This includes the Naval Base—one of the three world headquarters of NATO—and a Naval Air station.

Of all the naval sights, sounds and experiences that exist around Norfolk, one stands far above the others in impact—watching an aircraft carrier move through the harbor.

Driving along the road, idly scanning the skyline, you notice a most peculiar, thin skyscraper sticking up among the hotels and office buildings. A few moments later, you realize something is a bit odd. The thin skyscraper isn't in the proper perspective anymore. Why, if you didn't know better, you'd think the darn thing had moved.

You look closer and suddenly you realize that the building is moving. You pull off to the side of the road (carriers are more effective at getting motorists to do this than any police or ambulance siren) and stare. Then, realizing that it must be a carrier, you start the car and race toward the harbor, hoping for a good view. As you approach the Hampton bridge-tunnel or the harborside, the full ship swivels into view. Your first thought, straining your eyes to take in the entire enormity is, "Oh my God, it can't be real!"

It is not a ship, but a floating city. It looks as if a significant chunk of downtown has broken off and begun floating out to sea. The site is sobering and a little scary. The sense of steely power and purpose radiating from the giant vessel carries chilling whiffs of war. You are left with a mood that is a mixture of awe and repulsion.

One significant Army shrine augments the Naval presence predominating Norfolk—the burial place and museum of General Douglas MacArthur. Here are the corncob pipes, his many medals, his papers, even his limousine from the occupation in Japan. McArthur did not live in Virginia, but his family came from the Old Dominion, and he called it his "home by choice." In McArthur's museum, visitors can relive some of the daring exploits and incredible triumphs of the brilliant autocrat who has been called America's Caesar.

Langley Air Force Base, near Hampton, is America's oldest active military air installation. It's a sleek, slimmed down post, home of NASA's Langley Research Center, where America's space program was born. At Langley you see odd-shaped constructions used to delve into scientific problems of war and outer space. On the runways you spy needle-nosed jets of the most futuristic sort. Their job . . . who knows? But they look quietly deadly as they knife into the sky.

Nearby stands Fort Monroe, which, surrounded by a moat, is a genuine here-come-the-Indians fort in continuous use since 1819. The Army has a small contingent at Fort Monroe today, which regularly uncovers cannon balls, musket parts, and antique ammo left behind by earlier inhabitants.

Up north of Fredericksburg stands Quantico, a small but sinewy enclave of Marines. If we're ever invaded again, as in the War of 1812, these are the fellows who will defend Washington. Quantico's base is flanked by a shanty town of ramshackle homes and trailer courts. If it weren't for the gorgeous Virginia hills rising above everything, Quantico would look like a military base is supposed to: ribald, tacky and transient. The hills, however, give the place an incongruous sense of permanence.

The oddest military installation in the state is undoubtedly Mount Weather. All you see at this site west of Washington, is a long sloping hill and a fence. But beneath the surface lies the command center for America's government in time of attack. The bulk of the hill shields the center from a nuclear blast against the capital. It is an installation everyone involved hopes will never be fully used.

At Arlington National Cemetery, on a hill overlooking the Potomac and Washington—that was once the site of the Custis-Lee estate—lie thousands of Americans who have served their nation's armies. The stark white crosses laid against an emerald field are a sharp reminder of America's and Virginia's sufferings in the past.

On any afternoon you can stand on the hill at Arlington and look down on the sea of fallen soldiers. Here and there are families with small bunches of flowers which they lay upon the graves of their loved ones. And, down the hill comes the solemn procession of another soldier gone. He may have died in battle or he may have died in bed, but in his final moment wished to be remembered for his service in his prime. Taps is blown. Drums roll. Shots fire. The casket flag is folded smartly by the ramrod stiff honor guard and presented to the family. The wind blows through the trees.

Across from the cemetery stands the Pentagon, the world's largest office building, central nervous system of America's military. Officially, of course, the Pentagon doesn't lie in Virginia. In a flourish of executive privilege, the federal government annexed the land between the building and the river as part of the District of Columbia. But ignore the maps! Virginia claims the Pentagon as its own, except after major military fiascos. Then it reverts back to Washington's domination until the smoke clears.

The extensive military presence throughout the state has had substantial effects on Virginians. It has fed their natural conservatism. A state that is filled with soldiers tends not to be adverse to carrying a big stick in world affairs.

The military contingent has also forged a peculiar loyalty among the state's-rights minded Virginians for the Federal Government. Virginians see no problem with grousing about federal intrusion into their state at the same time they sing the praises of military expansion in the commonwealth.

Virginians tend to see patriotism in terms of supporting their country in war and strife. Hence, they feel perfectly comfortable accepting as many soldiers and military functions as Uncle Sam cares to send their way. In all other matters, though, Virginians see patriotism in terms of defending their state against the crackpot, corrupt, cancerlike intrusion of the Federal Government of their country.

The pragmatists in the Old Dominion point out with glee that a state economy based upon serving the military tends to be recession proof. And it's true that Virginia's unemployment runs well below national standards, and its general economic health has surpassed that of other southern states.

Why has Virginia become such an important military center? Because it offers innumerable advantages for the various services. Virginia features America's greatest natural harbor at Norfolk and has ample sources of water spread throughout the state. It also lures military planners by its proximity to Washington. The commonwealth sports a variety of terrain and excellent transportation facilities. In short, it has everything a military planner could want.

Driving down one of Virginia's Interstate highways on a typical afternoon, you're likely to see one of the long, pugnacious caravans of military vehicles heading from one base to another. Even when you know that war is not at hand, when your mind tells you the caravan is probably just delivering bread or fresh socks, seeing it rumble past gives your spine a little shiver.

Often, while lying on the beach or mowing the grass, a Virginian will look up to see squat, vicious-looking jets flying formation against the horizon. They look like deadly darts as they slide out of sight with unimaginable quickness.

Occasionally, a more direct interaction occurs. Once, I was driving the narrow country roads near my house in Skinquarter. I rounded a curve to come face to face with an imposing looking military roadblock. Soldiers stood all about, bristling with weaponry. Jeeps straddled the road. Radios squawked. Officers barked.

A soldier approached my car and told me I'd have to detour because of war games. My neighborhood, it appeared, had been chosen to substitute for a portion of Western Europe. Half miffed and half wild with curiosity, I drove along to the local store where, with other local denizens, I spent part of the afternoon watching soldiers wage World War III all over Virginia back roads.

It was better than a John Wayne movie, loud and exciting.

But the local hunters couldn't roust a deer for weeks afterward. Such are the wages of war.

The true price of war, though, is young lives. And Virginia has sent many sons into many wars. In addition, the sons of other states have passed through Virginia on their way to battle and back. Here, once again, is Walt Whitman with his poignant tribute to the lost young men of the Old Dominion:

As toilsome I wander'd Virginia's woods,
To the music of rustling leaves kick'd by my feet (for 'twas autumn),
I mark'd at the foot of a tree the grave of a soldier;
Mortally wounded he and buried on the retreat (easily all could I
   understand),
The halt of a mid-day hour when up! no time to lose—yet this sign left,
On a tablet scrawled and nail'd on the tree by the grave,
Bold, cautious, true, and my loving comrade.

Virginia Military Institute, the ramrod of commonwealth military tradition.

The launch of the nuclear attack sub *San Francisco* from Newport News.

Norfolk is home to the monsters of American defense, our city-sized aircraft carriers.

A joyous sailor from the carrier, U.S.S. *Nimitz*, shown above, in Norfolk harbor, swoops up his girlfriend after a tour in the Indian Ocean.

Glow from the boiler lights the face of a seaman on the U.S.S. *Hathaway* in Norfolk.

A soldier on maneuvers in Virginia needs water as much as in real combat.

Jets, like supersonic stilettos, await takeoff at Langley Air Force Base.

Wounded! Marines rush off a fallen comrade during mock war at Quantico.

The Roanoke funeral of Marine Sergeant John Davis who died in the
U.S. hostage rescue mission in Iran.

Crewmen of the U.S.S. *Eisenhower* wave good-bye as they leave for the troubled Middle East.

The
Water People

The water, in Virginia, isn't just the ocean side. Chesapeake Bay and its many fingers extend deeply into the heart of the commonwealth. In the bay, lie islands with unique customs and cultures. Along the bay shore, fishing and oystering communities extend nearly to Washington. From the bay, the rivers extend into the Piedmont, tying the great mass of Virginians to the sea—the Rappahannock, the Potomac, the Susquehanna and, most of all, the James have served as the essential arteries of Virginia growth and commerce for more than three hundred years.

The love affair between Virginians and their waters began at first sight. Captain John Smith was overwhelmed by the bounty of Chesapeake on his two 1608 explorations of the region. His excitement led him to make one of the first detailed maps of the bay. In 1612 he published a map along with a "Description" that rhapsodized about a new paradise: "Within is a country that may have the prerogative over the most pleasant places of Europe, Asia, Africa, or America, for large and pleasant navigable rivers: heaven and earth never agreed better to frame a place for man's habitation . . . Here are mountains, hills, plains, valleys, rivers and brooks all running most pleasantly into a faire Bay compassed but for the mouth with fruitful and delightsome land."

Over the years, the natural splendor of the Chesapeake region has won over everyone who has experienced it. With the sole exception, that is, of Captain Christopher Newport. He, poor fellow, was charged by the king to find a route through Virginia to the Pacific. He held high hopes for the Chesapeake, and it failed him. The bay's beauty gave him cold comfort.

Indeed, the bay is strikingly beautiful: richly blue, gently rolling, hauntingly fragrant. It is also vast. At its mouth the bay looks like the edge of a second ocean. The rivers running off it are the size of lakes. Even some of the creeks emptying near the outlet of the Chesapeake are several miles wide. Though the rivers and creeks narrow quickly as they head uphill into the state's heartland, the bay remains impressively wide all the way into Maryland.

The sheer size of the bay might have something to do with the inordinate possessiveness Virginians have for their coast, and for the ocean in general. After all, isn't it fair to assume a certain proprietary right when so great a chunk of inland ocean lies surrounded by Virginia?

Whatever the cause, Virginians do tend to think of the rest of the Atlantic seaboard as a suburb of the Virginia coast. "The ocean currents run all up and down, sure," a fellow from the eastern shore once told me, "but they like passing here best, which is why they're always so peaceful and pleasant as they goes by."

Virginia's watery territoriality extends to recreational invasions of the bay and coast with boats of all descriptions on any decent afternoon. Skiffs bob beside the shoreline reeds hoping for fish. Pencil-thin sailboats tilt and shift in the breeze. Motorboats race about with their pointy noses stuck in the air and lithe waterskiers splayed out behind. And cruisers redolent of tanning oil and mint juleps slide by with insouciant ease.

But the commonwealth's relationship with its waterways runs far deeper than recreation. The waters have added immeasurably to the Virginia character. They have also given the state much of its history and its geographical organization. Most Virginia cities stand where they do because of the Chesapeake and its rivers. Here, for instance, is how William Byrd II described the initiation of Richmond and Petersburg:

> When we got home, we laid the foundations of two large cities, one at Shaccos, to be called Richmond, and the other at the point of the Appomattox River, to be named Petersburg.... The truth of it is, these two places being the uppermost landing of James and Appomattox rivers, are naturally intended for marts, where the traffice of the outer inhabitants must center. Thus, we do not build castles only, but also cities in the air.

Jamestown became an early center of American life because it sat on the vital James River. Later, it lost influence when its position was found too open to attack down the very river that had spawned it. Fredricksburg came into existence as a hometown for seamen, and the downtown still bears the unmistakable imprint of the whalers, sailors and privateers.

Beyond geography, the flow of water through Virginia life has transferred to the state's people a deep, innate sense of the interplay of nature and the constancy of change. Virginians tend to be natural ecologists—especially those that live close to the waters.

Along Virginia shores you can still see many signs of the past: wrecked forts, Civil War vintage factories, old rail yards, the deserted docks of the steam packets that no longer ply the James, here and there the flat-top hump that denotes the tell of a lost Indian village. You can see, hear and smell the natural world. In their middle reaches Virginia's waters have become subject to modern environmental ills, but in the hills and along the bay, nature still wins out. Frogs croak, fish break the water leaping for flies, birds cry out and the waves lap softly against the hard shore.

In Virginia's water areas you can still feel the passage of natural seasons. Spring comes with a thrill of green through the somber reeds, and mist in the mornings. Summer brings squalls followed by late afternoons of etched gold light that bounces off the placid water. In fall, the shores become studies in chromatic brown and red, the water darkens and birds are active all around. In winter, there is fog and silence. Boats creak at their moorings and far across the water a single gull cries out.

Surrounded by such sights and sounds, Virginians become attuned to nature. They like to go down to the water and just sit. They like it as much in the chill, quiet winter as the humid busy summer. Virginia's waters are the neighborhoods her people visit to commune with the living world.

The waters have filtered into Virginia's commerce, too. Many Virginians fish or oyster for a living. Far more still spend their days building the world's largest ships to float on the nearby sea.

From the lower end of Gloucester, oystermen still rise before dawn and head into the bay at first light. They are weathered, stocky fellows who ply their trade in weathered, stocky ships. Their faces are seamed and rough, eroded by the salt winds and foggy damp.

Like all workers in harsh occupations, they joke unmercifully. Their humor tends toward tartness and their speech has a musical lilt, reminiscent of their heritage. Many are the descendants of Welsh sailors whose ships foundered off the coast.

The Chesapeake has always yielded a bounty of oysters. The first contact the Cape Henry settlers had with Indians was meeting a band on the beach roasting oysters they had simply scooped up from the water. Today's commercial oystermen use great tongs to scrape the shallow bottoms for the muddy shellfish. Their instinct for where the best beds lie is preternatural. They can't explain how the ability develops or what its criteria are. But they can always point out the fellow who has it.

That intuitive edge is becoming more and more necessary for oystermen, because human foolishness is destroying Virginia's oyster beds. Pollution spewed into the bay and inflowing rivers makes it impossible for the oysters to spawn or renders the adults foul tasting and unhealthy. The recent kepone disaster closed the entire James River to oystermen for quite some time, leaving Virginians to wonder how long the kepone disaster had existed before it was discovered, and what other tragedy might still remain hidden in the bay's waters. Another kepone disaster could kill the oystering enterprise in Virginia.

Crabbing is another serious occupation around the bay. When the early settlers arrived in Virginia they routinely found crabs the size of footballs. Today, such mammoth beasts are rare, but Chesapeake Bay blue crabs remain a popular delicacy and a significant coastal business.

In the bay-side rivers, crabs are taken with a line. This is simply a stout cord as much as a quarter-mile long. Every few feet a piece of salt-fish bait is knotted into the cord. Weights are placed at the ends and bouys (usually just a gallon can) are tied just back from the ends. The line is sunk, left and later reeled in. A wire dipnet is used to lift the feeding crab from the line.

In the bay proper, commercial crabbers use crab pots. These are so effective at catching the clawed creatures that their use is restricted. A crab pot is a two-cubic-foot chicken-wire box. The lower half is a bait compartment, the upper half the trap. Crabs enter to get the bait through funnel-shaped openings. Once inside they can only get out by heading into the upper chamber, where they are stuck until the trap is hauled in and opened.

Down the bay's peninsula from the oystering towns lie the bases of the huge commercial fishing fleets that ride out from Virginia to scour the mid-Atlantic coast. In armadas of large, swift trawlers they cruise far from shore, searching for schools of shimmering, squirming profit.

Perhaps the most exciting of these commercial fishing expeditions is following the run of the menhaden. The menhaden ships sail in midsummer and sometimes spend as much as a week at sea, hunting up and down for the racing herd of fish.

(Spotters sit high in the towers scanning the horizons.) When one cries out a sighting, the ships pounce like a racing military squad. Nets fly out. Ships drive and circle. The world becomes a dazzle of foam and fish and frothing white nets. Tons of fish are dragged to the decks in a matter of moments. The air is buffeted with sound.

After the holds are stuffed, the ships race back to port to unload. Their crews get a brief breather, then head out to do it all again. When the fish are running, no time can be lost!

Virginia's commercial fishing, once a family trade like oystering, has become largely corporate over the past decade. The ships now sail under the auspices of food conglomerates, cat-food companies and seafood contractors. The crews are more professional and less colorful than they might once have been. But there remains about them the essential toughness, irreverence and swagger of seamen. They still force the sea to yield to their skill and stamina even if their paycheck now comes in the mail from Houston or New York.

Life in partnership with the sea creates many more occupations than fishing. Over the years, the bay area has seen ropemakers, coopers, carvers, navigators and ironmongers come and go. The shipbuilders have been here since the beginning, too, and they remain.

Newport News Shipbuilding and Dry Dock Co. is the world's largest privately owned shipyard and the largest private employer in Virginia. It stretches for miles along the waterfront, an expanse of unbelievably huge docks, strange looking equipment, massive cranes and offices. Ugly, hot, smoky, but above all else, extremely powerful.

At Newport News, America builds its mightiest ships—aircraft carriers, nuclear submarines, mammoth tankers. The nuclear carriers *Nimitz* and *Eisenhower,* among others, were built here.

The workers at the shipyard are tough, sinewy people. Their jobs are hard, noisy, dangerous and dirty. They weld, pound steel, lift tremendous loads and balance against the thin skin of an emerging ship hundreds of feet above the ground. They don't have the natural, timeless life of the seagoing workers. They work on the schedule of industrial booms and busts. When ships need to be built, they have work. When contracts go elsewhere, they often have to sit and watch their money run out. This life makes for hard, uncompromising people. They work hard, play hard, live hard. They want every experience at the extreme because life is so uncertain. They have a constant, inner passion beneath their rough, stoic exteriors.

At the other extreme, in keeping with the Virginian penchant for holding onto the good things of the past, stand the craftsmen who build ships by hand. Several dozen men around the bay carry on this careful, complicated tradition. They no longer build the schooners and whalers of commercial fame; now they settle for pleasure boats and yachts. But the craft remains much the same. In order to make sure that the boatbuilders art remains alive, Norfolk, in 1978, opened a formal school of boatbuilding at Chessie Pier B at the foot of Brooke Avenue. Some sixty students are lead through the intricacies of the old art by builders from the bay region who still ply their trade. Nor is the school merely an outlet for hobbyists; the goal is to produce working shipwrights who will get jobs around the bay.

Among the bay area's shipbuilders, the most striking might be August F. Crabtree, and not just because he continues to build ships in his seventies, but because he crafts them at $1/48$ of their ordinary size.

Crabtree's miniature ships are masterpieces of workmanship. He builds them board by board, using the original plans. He uses scaled down tools, including one homemade chisel only $1/2000$-inch wide. Over a four-decade career Crabtree has crafted eighteen boats, from a Roman grain ship to a Cunard luxury liner. Sixteen of his ships are on display in Norfolk's Maritime Museum.

Norfolk and Virginia Beach, most of all, owe their position and success to the sea. Norfolk sits beside the greatest natural harbor in America. Its forty-five-foot deep channel has held the biggest boats of every age since discovery. Today, nuclear aircraft carriers ply the deep water.

It's a naval town, with a long tradition of swaggering sailors and their floating armed cities. When America has gone to war the ships have sailed from Norfolk. When war has come to America, Norfolk has often been the first place hit.

And, Norfolk people take a perverse pride in their military scars. One in particular, brings out the most boastful in local folk. St. Paul's Episcopal, an otherwise mild-mannered old building, has a fat cannonball wedged in a side wall. This, you are told, was hurled at the church by the ship of Lord Dunmore, Virginia's last royal governor, as he fled the rising tide of patriotism on New Year's Day 1776. Dunmore flattened every building in town but the church. Norfolkians like to point out that "m'Lord's aim was so poor he almost missed the church entirely."

Norfolk is a bustling, muscular sea town. Even the buildings seem to lean toward the ocean. But it is diversifying. The downtown area, once quite seedy, has been uplifted in the past few years by the addition of the Scope Convention Center, the Omni International Hotel complex and the stunning Chrysler Hall for the Performing Arts. And down by the waterfront, where sailors once fought and hootchie-kootchie girls wiggled, there now stands a lovely, landscaped mall, where office workers lunch and lovers stroll.

The naval personnel, while still an important force in the community, are being joined by increasing numbers of retirees, pleasure boat lovers and refugees from the big cities of the North. Norfolk is Virginia's dominant city today and will certainly grow more important in the years ahead.

Right down the road from Norfolk, Virginia Beach lies along the sweetest stretch of shimmering white beach north of Florida. It has been called "Virginia's Main Street," an apt description since it seems that every single family in the commonwealth tries to get there on sunny summer Sundays. The traffic jam approaching this sandy Mecca has taken on epic proportions, but once you get there, the wait seems worth it.

For twenty-nine miles the sand sweeps along the oceanside. It is never narrow, never rocky. Hiking up the beach you pass little old ladies in long sleeves beneath broad umbrellas, rubbery children wrestling each other across the sand, gaggles of office workers from Richmond with little on beside sun-tan oil, young families with picnic lunches and portable radios—a microcosm of the state, and so, a microcosm of the country.

Virginia Beach, like many resort areas, has two populations— the summer folk and the townies. Virginia Beach townies are shockingly friendly. They don't even seem to mind that their pretty town and gorgeous beach are mauled by hordes from the inner precincts. Perhaps this is because virtually everyone who lives in Virginia Beach makes his living from these visitors.

What is even odder about Virginia Beach folk is that they stay friendly during off season. In Estes Park, Colorado, and other such spots, I have always found the townies to become positively surly when the tourists leave. But in Virginia Beach, the townies seem even friendlier when the pressure is off than they do during the summer.

And Virginia Beach in wintertime is something special, at least for me. The beach so vivid and hot in summer becomes a foggy, mysterious bourne in winter. The waterside hike is more conducive to valuable introspection, romance and peace than any other walk I've taken. It is quiet all about. The sea laps at the dark, cold shore. The birds stir in the misty air. Your breath hangs frosty in the salt air. You go back to your warm hotel, wolf down a huge seafood dinner and sleep like a baby.

The most unique community around the bay is surely the isolated island fastness of Tangier Island. In 1609 six English families settled this tiny flat island in the heart of the Chesapeake. They are still there, and only twelve new families have joined them.

Far from any shore, the small population on this island has evolved a unique culture. Islanders still speak as their ancestors did, in a colonial argot that sounds more cockney than American. They have married cousins so frequently that whispers can be heard about the bleeding disease, hemophelia, appearing in some of the children. They make their living as they always have, by crabbing and fishing. Only the fellow who runs the state-maintained airport and the local policeman don't go out with the boats. All their goods come from shore on the daily mail boat, or through day-long hoarding excursions by islanders to the mainland. They bury their dead above ground, often in their front yards, because land is scarce and you can't dig down two feet on Tangier without hitting water.

There are no cars on Tangier. Everyone walks, bikes or mopeds. Mothers turn their kids outside with confidence because they can't get hurt in traffic. Old, old clapboard houses line the curving, narrow streets. The families living in them are usually as old as the houses. The young folks will live there from birth well past marriage, because someone has to die before a house opens up they can buy.

Tangier's special way of life draws tourists by the boatload. In summer, two tourist boats a day drop five hundred gawkers on the island. The island's native population is only eight hundred. Unlike other attractive spots, Tangier ignores its visitors. Only a couple of islanders make money from them. The rest hold them in mild contempt. They don't like being stared at, and they're tired of questions about feeble-mindedness through inbreeding.

One old islander tells the story of turning that prejudice back into a tourist's face:

"Fellow comes along and sees me out back feedin' my chickens. So he asks me what I'm doin'. Now, that's a damn dumb thing to ask anybody So, I told him I was feedin' my dogs.

"He looked for a minute and said, 'How many dogs you got?' "

"I told him, I got a dozen—oh, wait a minute—I only got eleven. We ate one for supper last night."

Tangier is a God-fearing, churchgoing community. A non-churchgoer would be ostracized. Drinking is proscribed on the island, but the local gents do have a loophole. The crabbing men all have small shacks sitting offshore. Here they clean their catches and store them in baskets for taking to market. Called crab shanties or crab houses, many a Tangier wife often hears that there's 'a might load of work at the shanty today. Of course, in addition to the crabbing supplies, the shanties are stocked high with potables. The shacks serve as offshore social clubs, allowing the menfolk to have their snort while preserving the official policy that "there is no booze *on* Tangier Island."

The closest thing to an unhappy group on Tangier Island are the teenagers. They're bored and hemmed in. The island has no amusements. The one restaurant is largely for tourists. There are no cars for kids to race around in. They migrate to the island's small footbridges and stand around on summer nights staring at the water.

On a tiny, jam-packed island, you can find no lovers lanes, and everybody knows your business. So teen romance is a rough commodity on Tangier. Going to the mainland, except for special occasions, is out of the question. The kids will marry young and get to work for lack of anything else to do.

Tangier feels and sounds like a community from a hundred years ago. The people would certainly have more in common with a nineteenth-century New Bedford whaling captain than a contemporary urban American.

On the rare times Tangier Islanders visit the big city, they flummox the locals. One island woman tells the story of her visit to New York:

"I was in a taxi marveling at seeing New York, and the cabbie asked me where I was from. He said, 'I know you must be English.' I said I was from Tangier Island, Virginia, in Chesapeake Bay. He got angry. He said, 'Quit lying to me, I know you're from England!' Finally, in order to get out of the cab I had to say, 'You're right, I am from England.' It was the only lie I've ever told."

Dry humor and salty self-reliance run richly through the personality of Virginia's water people. They demonstrate many of the qualities traditionally associated with New Englanders—laconic honesty and clanishness, to name just two. So, perhaps these traits are more a product of the sea than the surroundings. Unlike New Englanders, though, the folks along Virginia's waterways exude a reckless frontier spirit that is far spicier than anything you'd find up North. Coastal Virginians have a broad streak of roustabout in them.

Take the Chincoteague pony round up, for instance. Once a year, the sober volunteer firemen of this bustling bay island become watery range riders as they drive wild ponies across the channel from uninhabited Assateague Island. Descended from horses that swam ashore following shipwrecks hundreds of years ago, the ponies must be kept in check or the Assateague herd will become too large to survive.

But the water folks have built a singular spectacle from the simple process. Whooping and hollering, the cowboy bay dwellers charge the wide-eyed horses into the surf. The short channel between the islands fills with bobbing twisting horses, wreathed in white plumes of spray.

On the Chincoteague side, herded by the once-a-year buckaroos, they gallop along the main street to the city park. Crowds line the path roaring at the show. And, in the park, they bid on the ponies at an enormous horse auction. Many a Virginia child has gotten a desperately desired pony from the Chincoteague sale.

Water folk, as Chincoteague's round-up shows, like to do things in a big, brawling way. When folks along the coast got tired of hearing about all the snazzy civic events in other parts of the state, they refused to be topped. Instead, they founded the Urbanna Clam Fest, which could easily qualify as the greatest gorging available in modern America.

The steaming heaps of clams, corn on the cob, beans and Brunswick stew boggle the mind. The air is heavy with savory smoke and steam. Beer flows freely—some say too freely. And a level of animated craziness pushes the festivities forward. It is a celebration of life, of people and of natural bounty.

The self-reliance of water folk sometimes hardens into unshakeable stubbornness, even cussedness. In Arlington on the eastern shore (this is the original, the town in northern Virginia stole the name), there stands the grave of John Custis, which reads:

> Aged 71 years
> and Yet, liv'd but Seven Years which
> was the space of time He kept a Batchelers
> house at Arlington on the Eastern Shore
> of Virginia

Even in death, Custis couldn't keep from reminding his detested wife, Frances, just how much he disliked her. In life, the two of them matched each other in cussedness. After years of mutual berating they stopped speaking. Each would direct his comments at their slave, Pompey, who would carry the message to the other. Then, for reasons unknown, Custis took his wife for a carriage ride one day.

According to local legend he was determined to get her to talk to him. So, he drove the carriage across the sand and into the bay. As water gushed in the sides, Mrs. Custis looked over cooly and asked,

"Where are you going, Colonel Custis?"

"To hell, Madam," her bitter husband replied.

Unruffled she retorted with: "Then, drive on. Any place is better than Arlington."

His bluff called, Custis headed back to shore. "Madam," he grumbled, "I believe you would as soon meet the Devil himself if I should drive to Hell."

Again, his wife topped him. "Sir," she replied, "I know you so well I would not be afraid to go anywhere you would go."

Speaking of local legends, here is one that has tantalized shore wanderers for more than 230 years. In 1750 a convict named Charles Wilson tried to smuggle a note to a friend. His jailers intercepted it. They immediately took off to try and solve the mystery it posed, but without success. Many others have tried and failed since. Was it just a joke on the jailers, or is it true? Read Wilson's instructions, and decide for yourself:

> There are three creeks lying 100 paces or more north of the second inlet above Chincoteague Island, Virginia, which is at the southward end of the peninsula. At the head of the third creek to the northward is a bluff facing the Atlantic Ocean with three cedar trees growing on it, each about one-and-a-half yards apart. Between the trees I buried ten iron-bound chests, bars of silver, gold, diamonds and jewels to the sum of 200,000 pounds sterling. Go to Woody Knoll secretly and remove the treasure.

Of course, an impediment to finding Wilson's treasure today is the extensive change that has occurred along the bay shore. His cedar trees are probably plowed under a housing development by now. The accelerating pace of change along Virginia's waters, in fact, threatens to destroy the natural balance and life style found there.

Population around the bay will double by the year 2020, to some 16 million, according to the Army Corp of Engineers Chesapeake Bay Study Group. The small fishing villages may be swallowed up by growing recreational suburbs. Increased freshwater requirements for all these people, and accompanying industry, will reduce flow into the bay, increasing its salinity and possibly wreaking havoc with seafood life cycles.

And the bay will get dirtier. Urbanization upstream is already taxing Chesapeake Bay—and not just from Virginia. "It's not well understood," says David Flemmer, who runs the Federal Environmental Protection Agency's Chesapeake project, "that the bay is a coupled system, coupled to the uplands. The headwaters of the Susquehanna are in New York, and we're dealing with the Chesapeake Bay as the backwater of the Catskills. Many of the materials in the bay come down from the uplands."

Both the matchless plentitude and the increasing perils to the bay came home to me in a visit a couple years back to a friend's homestead on the Eastern Shore. The ramshackle farmhouse stood far back from any road. Its location made sense only in terms of water, not land. Out the backdoor to the right was a fresh-water pond, fed by underground springs. Clams literally crunched underfoot as you waded into it. Getting dinner required merely enough stooping and scraping to fill the clam bucket.

Out back and to the left lay an inlet from the bay. Poles propped up along the shore had caught some fish, which my friend and I collected and carried up to the house. Our work with the poles disturbed ducks who erupted from the rushes in a squawking ferment. The air smelled tangy with salt and rich with the aroma of sea life and greenery. At the time I told my friend that my notion of heaven was something like this.

A week later my friend called on the edge of hysteria. She had awoken that morning to find the world turned black. An oil tanker had illegally bilged its tanks offshore. The gook had ridden in on the tide. The beach was a mass of ooze. The inlet was coated with gunk, in which the bodies of dead fish floated. A macabre bouillabaisse.

Blackened ducks stumbled around, dazed, like the survivors of an air raid. My friend had spent the whole day struggling against their feeble protests as she tried to wash them clean. And crying when they died in her arms.

Virginia has crafted a unique and lovely civilization along her shore. It has vigorously withstood three centuries of development and change. But the life-style and the area have grown so fragile their specialness could vanish in a generation. So, cherishing them now, becomes more important than ever.

145

A Newport News dockworker, with a demeanor as tough as the chains he winches.

A shipbuilder at Newport News, whose shining eyes express satisfaction with his work.

There is nothing on earth so satisfying as a successful day of fishing.

I know it's not a big fish, but's it's the best I could do.

Picket Larry Chidress makes his displeasure known as workers enter the Newport News Shipbuilding Yard during a recent strike to win union representation by the United Steelworkers of America.

Like an alien invader, a ship welder peers at the world from beneath his protective hood.

Tangier Island in winter looks like a miniature town floating on a frozen lake. Ties with the mainland are kept clear by the hard work of the Coast Guard cutters.

Mrs. Euna Dise poses outside her boardinghouse that puts up hundreds
of Tangier visitors yearly.

One of Virginia's biggest thrills is running the James River rapids.

The opening of the fifth annual Norfolk Harborfest: the parade of tall ships.

Netting herring in the shallows near Franklin, Virginia.

Hanford Crosure, Richmond's harbormaster, epitomizes the tenacity and character of Virginia's water people in his fight against decay and pollution.

The Agrarians

Midwestern farms are vast and businesslike. Pennsylvania farms are tribal, with hex signs and distinctive architectural style. Virginia farms are varied, each different type reflecting the character of its region and crop.

Down in Southside are the tobacco farms. The land is flat and marked by clumps of forest that separate the small fields. Each field is filled with tobacco plants that look like big green hats from a Dr. Suess book. Not an inch is wasted; the plants all but overlap and run right to the edge of the road.

The sensation is that of a roiling, dark green sea, broken by thick islands of trees.

And then there are the curing sheds, low and ramshackle, colored dusky red or faded green. They always seem to be surrounded by high weeds; and appear a bit swaybacked, as if they've been worked too hard for years and are ready for pension. You can see the racks of leaves through spaces around the lopsided door. And the sweet, alcoholic smell lies heavy in the humid air.

Tobacco farmhouses tend toward sturdy old frame structures, with lots of additions patchworked on, as the kids were added and the generations grew. You find them back in the woods, down by the creek, with a hammock and a pile of cordwood in the front yard and a couple wrecked trucks out back.

In the upper Piedmont and Shenandoah foothills you find the big, working crop farms. Their checkered fields of yellow, gold and many shades of green, wrap around the hills and valleys in all directions as far as the eye can see. Here are acres of wheat and corn, soybeans and clover. The fields are crisp, neat and incredibly rich, like a thick carpet laid at the foot of the mountains.

On a hillcrest stands the house, a good stone building surrounded by trees generations old, and so huge that only the chimneys can be seen above the leaves. The barn lies in the hollow, a low hump of corrugated metal or perhaps a narrow building of weathered slats, with a steeply canted roof. In the yard stand the huge, buglike implements of major mechanical farming.

(The scene says, "this is a prosperous place. Life here is generous and hospitable.")

Farther up the slopes lie the apple orchards: Swales and hollows of squat trees, their arthritic limbs heavy with fruit. They don't look so much like farms as parks. Most people's image of Elysium probably looks something like a Shenandoah orchard: To lie in the soft sun, in the shadow of the dark green hills, head against a gnarled root, legs splayed out in the smooth grass. Pick a little fruit, drink a little wine. Omar Khayam would approve.

But these orchards are working farms. Their crop is important to the state. So, mechanical fruit pickers and bug sprayers move among the trees. Workers carefully prune and tend them. And at harvest semi-trailers stand at the orchard edge, to be filled with mind boggling loads of ripe fruit.

Of all Virginia farms, though, the quintessential image comes from the horse farms of the Blue Ridge. These are the descendants of Virginia's great plantations. They speak of ease, grandeur and history as much as of husbandry.

The first view of a horse farm is always the fence. Not some two-bit barbed wire number, but a stunningly white board barrier that edges the road and runs off into the fields and paddocks. How, one wonders, can they ever keep the thing painted? How did they ever get all those miles of fence erected? It must have taken generations. Exactly. The fence is a symbol that this is no new operation; it's been around awhile and done quite well for itself, thank you.

Next comes the driveway. There may be pillars of smoky colored brick, or a tall iron gate. There may simply be an understated RFD box. But always there is the thin macadam curving back into the trees toward a house that can barely be seen from the road.

And the houses themselves, of course, are pillared, chimneyed, porticoed exemplars of colonial design made modern. In town such a building would be the Elks Club or City Hall, but out here it is part home, part office and part shrine. It says: We can be modern and still live as well as our ancestors did.

Around this evocative scene gallop the sleek, shiny thoroughbreds and their wobbly legged foals. The scene is timeless and mesmerizing. An undiminished ideal of American rural life.

Virginians have always been a rural people. Thomas Jefferson had enormous respect for farmers. He called them "the chosen people of God," and ever since his day Virginians have held agrarian pursuits in high esteem.

Jefferson also said that the study of plants represented "the most valuable sciences, whether we consider its subject as funneling the principal substance of life to man bearing delicious varieties for our tables, refreshments from our orchards, the adornments of our flowers, borders, shades and perfumes from our groves, materials for our buildings or medicaments for our bodies."

The dream of all true Virginians is to retire to the country, to raise a small crop and a few horses, to swing on the porch at night and listen to the crickets and the rustle of leaves.

And yet, farming is also one of Virginia's biggest industries. Farmers represent one of the most potent economic forces in the state. In addition to tobacco, Virginia deals in poultry, peanuts, apples, even cattle. For many Virginians, life centers on what happens in the fields.

But not for as many as it used to. Virginia's farm population has dropped steadily through this century. In 1920, 300,000 people worked the land, but by 1970 that number had dropped to 53,000. Some of this is the result of more efficient farming methods, but a lot of it stems from the loss of farmland to urban sprawl and the inability of small, independent farmers to stay in business.

In addition, the reduction of their numbers has decreased farmers' impact on state government. Once the country folk could rest assured that their majority in the legislature would protect their interests. But a 1962 reapportionment recognizing the growth of the cities shifted the political majority away from the farmers. Appomattox State Senator Charles T. Moses groaned in frustration: "The reins of government should rest in the hands of those that turn the soil and slop the hogs!"

A famous tale shows that even in colonial times Virginia was considered important primarily for its crops. A delegation of colonists led by James Blair went to England to seek funds for Virginia's first college and seminary. The king and queen were amenable, but crusty Attorney General Edward Seymour had his doubts. Virginia needed trained ministers, Blair argued in an audience with Seymour. Their souls needed saving, too.

"Souls!" bellowed Seymour. "Damn your souls! Make Tobacco!"

The importance of tobacco in Virginia's development and commerce can't be overstressed. As Virginia Moore puts it: "Virginia reeks of tobacco. Its odor saturates her like the coat of a veteran smoker. The brown stain of tobacco is on every page of her history."

Dr. Joseph C. Robert of the University of Richmond has called the successful cultivation of tobacco "the most momentous single fact in the first century of settlement on the Chesapeake Bay. . . . It guaranteed the permanence of the Virginia settlement; created the pattern of the Southern plantation; encouraged the introduction of Negro slavery, then softened the institution; strained the bonds between mother country and the Chesapeake colonies; burdened the diplomacy of the post-Revolutionary period; promoted the Louisiana Purchase; and, after the Civil War, helped create the New South."

Virginians, however, cannot take credit for introducing the sweet smoking leaf to the world. Christopher Columbus deserves that honor. He found the Indians smoking away when he first got here, and brought word of the strange, ceremonial weed back to Europe with him. In 1535 a fellow named Francisco Fernandez brought a plant to Philip II of Portugal. Jean Nicot, French Ambassador to Portugal, sent some of its seeds to Catherine de Medici, Queen of France. His gift so delighted the court that it became known as nicotine.

Sir Walter Raleigh introduced the plant to Queen Elizabeth I, and later got to smoke a pipeful of it before James I cut off his head. In time, tobacco became quite the rage among European intellectuals and the demand for the stuff grew to a clamor. Europe turned ravenously to the colonies for tobacco, and in Jamestown John Rolfe had the bright notion that instead of trading with the Indians for tobacco his colonists could grow it themselves.

Captain John Smith thought this idea disgusting, but the lust in Europe for tobacco and in the colonies for a cash crop prevailed. Boom! The economy of the colonies—and Virginia in particular—exploded in a burst of tobacco pipe smoke. The money and power growing in their fields gave colonists a taste to wrest control of their own affairs. One wonders about the course of American freedom if Europeans had been able to curb their desire for soothing smoke.

Tobacco became the colonies' first native currency. Wages were figured in terms of pounds of tobacco. Wealth was figured on the basis of a man's tobacco holdings. And, of course, in short order the demands of tobacco farming spurred the introduction of slavery to the colonies. In a real sense, the resulting Civil War saw the American union go up in smoke.

Virginia has always presented the perfect environment for growing tobacco. The soil is rich and the climate is mild and moist. From the 1600s fields and ramshackle curing barns have covered the state—and still do. On their heels have come the manufacturing facilities of America's huge cigarette industry, a continuing boon to Virginia's economy. Except for the interruptions of war, the love affair between Virginia and tobacco hasn't waned since colonial times.

Today, Virginia has a tobacco industry worth more than $5 billion a year. Tobacco fields line the roadsides for miles in southeast and south central parts of the state. The squat, droopy plants following one after another, row on row, look like an army of green Carmen Miranda hats.

Tobacco warehouses and curing barns fill the wrong-side-of-the-tracks neighborhoods of many a Virginia city. South Richmond is an example: "In South Richmond," wrote Tom Robbins in his novel *Even Cowgirls Get the Blues,* "the mouse holes, lace curtains and Sears catalogs, even the baloney sandwiches and measles epidemics, always wore a faint odor of cured tobacco."

At harvest time, teams of pickers with long bags, worn hands and stooped backs still head into the fields to pick the ripe leaves, often called "preclow stink." A machine can't yet look at a tobacco leaf and tell when it's ripe. A person has to do it, looking for the right texture and pattern or characteristic yellow spots on the leaf.

Then comes the tobacco auction. The auctioneer, generally a short, portly fellow in a striped shirt, white trousers and shoes, wearing a hat indoors, meets the buyers at the warehouse door. Behind him range rows of baled tobacco, filling the huge room with their sleepy, sweet smell.

At a slow, steady pace the auctioneer sets off among the rows. His hands mark the beat of his call as he moves from bale to bale. He makes a constant flow of sound, a hypnotic chant of whaddayas and gottayas, utterly incomprehensible to an outsider, clear as rain to the buyers. With small hand signals and nods they make their bids and buy their burley. Then, the chant moves along to the next allotment.

It's interesting to note, by the way, that for all his praise of farmers, Thomas Jefferson hated the cultivation of tobacco, which he characterized as "a culture productive of infinite wretchedness. Those employed in it are in a continual state of exertion beyond the power of nature to support. Little food of any kind is raised by them; so that the men and animals on these farms are illy fed and the earth is rapidly impoverished."

The land, happily, has always managed to replenish itself from tobacco's drains, but some of the farmers have not. It has become increasingly difficult for Virginia farmers to survive.

Walter L. "Pete" Ellis is a tall, rangy fellow with a shaggy gray beard and a mop of curly salt-and-pepper hair. He farms more than 800 acres in Sussex County near the Nottoway River. Pete is the unofficial leader of the farmers in his area, and he's just about ready to throw in the towel.

"If the agricultural situation doesn't get any better," he says, "I'll have to get out. I'll have no other choice." And, Ellis points out, when he does, so will many others: "When Pete Ellis goes, there will be a lot of others giving up, too. And we are about at the end of our endurance. We are not making any money. We can't put anything aside for a cushion."

Rising land values, which push taxes ahead of them, are making it hard for farmers to hang onto their land. The pressure to keep prices down for consumers makes it hard for tobacco farmers to get the money they need to stay afloat. So, each year more and more jump overboard.

Still, in Virginia it's true that you can take the man from the farm but not the farm from the man. Weekend farmers abound. Common is the pinstriped vice-president who can barely wait through the week to jump back into his overalls and go mess in the dirt. During the summer, city dwellers rent plots on the outskirts of town so they can plant a decent-sized crop. Those who can't afford that will fill their postage stamp back yards with tomatoes and beans and greens. The urge to husband runs deep through the state.

Timber is another of Virginia's important agricultural resources. The state is abundantly forested. It produces Christmas trees, pulpwood, pine and hardwoods for the rest of America.

The state has aggressively supported this renewable, natural harvest. In one recent year, for example, Ablemarle County land-

166

owners received fifty million new baby trees from Virginia nurseries in New Kent and the Shenandoah Valley. In addition, more than 500,000 seedlings were planted in the county that year.

The new trees are important because the need for and production of timber from Virginia has grown steadily since early times. In 1820 Ablemarle had seventeen sawmills, which produced 900,-000 board feet of lumber. In 1977 the same county's twelve modern sawmills produced 14 million board feet in addition to untold thousands of cords of firewood.

Virginians have always taken their trees very seriously. Many Old Dominion homes are graced by huge old oaks, elms or ash trees that date from the Revolution. They are all but considered members of the family.

A famous story shows just how devoted Virginians can get to august old trees. An ash tree was planted at the University of Virginia in 1876. It was a normal tree, but it caught the fancy of a University English professor William A. McGuffey, the man who created the famous McGuffey reader that introduced many generations of Americans to their language.

All through his career, McGuffey tended the tree, until it became known, fittingly, as McGuffey's tree. Now, as time passed, a construction contractor decided that McGuffey's tree would have to be cut down to make room for a new building on campus. Outraged, Mrs. William E. Piles, the wife of a professor, propped a chair against the tree and would not budge until the contractor backed down and let the old tree stand.

Virginians also raise a lot of flowers, both for pleasure and profit. There is a Daffodil Festival in Gloucester, an Apple Blossom fest in Winchester and an azalea celebration in Norfolk. There's Garden Week in April, when so many flower gardens are opened for viewing by so many flower fanciers that it seems everyone in the state is either growing or going.

The abundance and variety of flowers are special by-products of Virginia's rich land and mild climate. Virginia Moore describes their role splendidly: "In Virginia the year is not so much a series of months as a procession of flowers: some expected, some arrived, some just fixing to depart. In February, before the frogs get exercised upon the coming of spring, you can find pure snowdrops under dark, mouldy, wet leaves, till blue and white striped crocuses put in an appearance and long legged daffodils, white narcissi rimmed narrowly with yellow, frank-colored tulips, lilacs that hoard the sweet rain, flags, roses and then my pets, flamboyant Oriental poppies with hairy leaves and great black stamens dusted with purple; and it is time to bury your enravished nose in sweet peas and keep it there till the zinnias and asters by the fence are competing with the goldenrod upon the hill."

But Virginians do not relate to the land only through plants. They still see the countryside as a hunting ground as well. Virginians love to hunt. They fill the woods and duck ponds during season, shooting at everything around, including each other.

Just after dawn on a crisp autumn day, the deer hunters tiptoe down the stairs, rev up the truck and head out for the prearranged meeting ground. It might be a parking lot, or somebody's particularly large driveway, but most likely it's just a bend in the road or a clearing large enough to hold the cars and trucks full of hunting dogs.

As the hunters arrive they form convivial groups around steaming thermoses of (often spiked) hot coffee. Their feet crunch on on the dirt in the spreading morning light, the dogs shuffle and howl in their pens. Doors slam. Laughs ripple outward.

Finally, enough boys are present for planning to commence. Somebody spreads out a map, or maybe just draws a diagram on the back of a piece of office letterhead. The crowd presses around, angling for a view, offering suggestions, disputing proposals for setting up the hunt.

"All right, Henry, you take your dogs and head on up here to the corner of the Hog Farm and you run 'em up toward Edgar's place over t'here. And Sam, you take some fellas and set up a line through these woods. I'll take my dogs over by the creek and work 'em back toward Henry. The rest of you boys fan out along these roads here. Now, how's that sound?"

The deer hunters work like military squads on patrol. They break into teams. They hide themselves in the branches of trees along predetermined flushing lines. They head into the woods with teams of dogs let loose at craftily chosen points. Then they wait. And wait. And wait.

Eventually, there'll be a whoop and a holler and a crash and one of the boys will come stumbling out of the woods with a nice seven-pointer slung across his shoulders. He's puffing like a steam engine and his eyes are so bright he could see in a closed closet without a flashlight. But the code of the woods requires that he be modest.

"Whoooe, Henry, that there's some deer. You must be tuckered hauling that monster over here."

"Naw, it weren't nothin'." Then, of course, he lifts his prize into the pick-up and collapses onto the tailgate.

Fowl hunters, on the other hand, work in small teams, like commandoes. They rise before dawn and position themselves at first light. They are armed to the teeth with tools of deception and camouflage. Hidden among the rushes along the bay or creek or river, they crouch, make bird calls, send out decoys. And wait and wait and wait.

Suddenly, with a squawk and a tremendous racket, birds break cover nearby. The hunter leaps up and fires away. His dog dives into the water and proudly returns with a soggy, ruffly-feathered trophy. And then the process begins again.

For the Virginians, of course, the heart of hunting isn't the kill. Getting a head to mount, a venison steak or a duck dinner is nice, but not vital. The real reason for hunting is the stories.

"I don't know, Henry. That deer's big, but I think George's big one last season was a mite larger."

"That puny thing? Why I distinctly remember he carried that itty-bitty creature back to camp slung over one arm. I recall we had to find the antlers with a magnifying glass . . ."

" . . . so there I was answering nature's call against a tree and I hear this crashing behind me . . ."

" . . . Whose dogs was it flushed that deer? Give them dogs some Alpo, those're fine animals, yes sir . . ."

The woods are like God's own social club for Virginians.

However, for a few folks, Virginia's rural areas are still a haven. The state has a smattering of Amish and Mennonites who live out their simple lives, undisturbed in the quiet country corners of Virginia. And in Louisa County a group of idealistic, dedicated young people have established a utopian community based upon the concepts in B. F. Skinner's *Walden Two*. At Twin Oaks everything is shared, and all decisions affecting the community are made in concert. They farm and run a few small businesses and lead their lives as they wish without interference. Other, individual back-to-the-landers have chosen Virginia's rural fastnesses for their attempts to return to the self-sufficient farm life of a century ago.

Whatever they may think of the beliefs of such unusual ruralites, Virginians as a whole respect them. As one farmer said, "Whatever else a man does or thinks, if he makes something come out of the land, you've got to give him his due. There ain't no work more fitting of respect."

Perhaps it is this attitude of respect for farming and the land that has lifted so many leading Americans from Virginia soil. And not only the well known names of Virginia history, but the leaders of other areas, as well.

The man who made Texas was one of these. Sam Houston was the fifth son of a farmer in Timber Ridge, Virginia. In 1807 his father died and Sam's mother, Elizabeth Paxton Houston, packed her family up and headed West into the wilderness. But Sam was already fourteen, a man by the standards of his time. The personality that would galvanize the Southwest and forge the largest state was formed on a Virginia farm.

So, too, was the character of Cyrus McCormick, a man who revolutionized farming. McCormick's Scotch-Irish family had migrated into the Valley of Virginia from Pennsylvania and prospered. They held 1,800 acres and ran mills for flour and timber.

Cyrus grew up on the land, working his family's farm. He learned firsthand the enormous struggle of the grain harvest and the cruelty of the weather if the harvest were taken in slowly. Though thinly educated, he was clever and began to muse about a machine that could take over the job.

McCormick tinkered in his father's blacksmith shop for years, developing his reaper. Finally, he demonstrated his invention in 1831 on the neighboring fields of John Steele. Virginia, though, after having developed McCormick, couldn't support him. His reaper did not catch on in the hilly farm country.

So, the young inventor headed West, where the land was vast and flat and men were hard to come by. He built his reaper factory in a nowhere spot at the edge of civilization—Chicago. Having left his native state behind, he played a central role in opening up the West and feeding the growing American populace.

The pull of tradition remains strong among Virginia's agrarians. Many farmers around the state still maintain teams of dray horses, the huge bulky beasts that once pulled all the plows. In most cases this is sentimental, a bow to tradition and the hard work of the old days. The farmers keep their teams in the barn except for special occasions.

But a few farmers go so far as to actually use the horses in the old way. John Redifer of Mt. Crawford, for instance, plows his farm with a two-horse team.

"I like to work with the horses," he says. "You can't talk to a tractor; can't reason with it. Horses don't break down, they don't gobble gas. They work hard and don't take much tending.

"I guess I'm just partial to the old ways. But horse farming seems to make sense to me. I wouldn't want to spend all my time fooling with machines."

Others keep a symbolic link to the past in their own fashion. Stephen Suggs, for instance, collects old carriages. He has more than two dozen carefully put away in a barn on his farm near Goochland. Everything from Conestogas to the ice wagons of his youth. He keeps them not so much for their material value, but as a reminder to himself of where true values lie and what should really be important to people.

"I want to preserve something of the old times," he explains, "because I think it's vital that we have something left of a period when things were a good deal healthier than they are now. I think the social fabric in our country is coming apart because we've lost touch with the land.

"We are out of touch with nature and we need to have the stability that nature offers, the sense of true life passing to be whole. I think its a tragedy that America seems to be leaving its land behind. It the only real important thing we've got."

Virginia's rural regions have their share of poor people. The rednecks and so-called poor white trash are found in Virginia, as in the rest of the South. But there's something different about Virginia, even here.

If there is anything about the rural poor that makes other people uncomfortable it's a chip-on-the-shoulder attitude toward everybody. A sneering, nasty outlook on life brought about by economic disadvantage. Although in Virginia you may find all the accoutrements of redneckism—beer, stock cars, busted old cars, sad guitar music, wild-eyed chauvanism, chewing tobacco, guns and old dogs—you won't find the meanness of the Deep South.

This is, it seems, because pocket money has never been the yardstick by which rural Virginians measured themselves. Worth arises from good storytelling, good farming, good religion, steadiness and support for your friends and family. Money's no big deal. If some folks want to lock themselves up in offices all day, miss out on all the good things the land offers, that's their right, but it doesn't make them any better. Not by a long shot.

Virginia's rural areas are undergoing forced change. The economics of farming are making it ever harder for the small, family farms to stay alive. The cities are spreading out, gobbling up farm land as they go. The quiet, land-centered Virginia rural life-style is being challenged by the problems and temptations of the modern media age. How, after all, are you gonna keep the next generation down on the farm, after they've seen "Kojak"?

The political clout of Virginia's rural expanses has diminished. Once the farmers ruled the state. Now the city folks do. The land used to have a value in and of itself. Now it is considered valuable for what can be done to it, how it can be developed.

Still, for all the shifting, in the words of Guy Fridell "This is still an agrarian land. The fields and forests, streams and silos, red barns and white ones, are made rich by the Valley's dramatic and colorful past history, and are dominated for eternity by the worn ancient hazy-blue hills which once held back an inland sea."

In places Virginia's land looks like a swirling sea broken by islands of trees.

Given the chance, most Virginians would like a back yard big enough for a barn and a tractor.

A young farmer in communion with his porcine business partners.

In rural Virginia, a hog dressing can become a family event.

Power, a Virginia politician once said, should be in the hands of those
who slop the hogs.

The cleansing. As the congregation looks on a young woman is baptized
in a small mountain creek.

Two Southside boys set in tobacco plants from the back of a dusty tractor.

Picking beans in the huge garden at Twin Oaks community in Pouisa County.

Virginians tend to take their gardening seriously.

Picking beans in the huge garden at Twin Oaks community in Pouisa County.

Virginians tend to take their gardening seriously.

Emily Galumbeck, with the help of Karen Carroll and her son Nathan, cans large amounts of home-grown tomatoes every summer.

An oldster and his young friend take a horse and buggy outing along rural roads near Chesapeake.

In Carrollton, a pair of horses huddle together like orphans of the storm.

An old farmhouse filled with tomato crates looks, for all the world, like a big mouth with ill-fitting dentures.

An aerial view of rich farmlands in the Piedmont.

The strength and solidity of the land seem to flow through the gaze of this Piedmont farmer.

Tough guy, sad songs, cold beer, eternal are the components of country life.

It's a still, all right, but this one is used to make gasohol.

Virginia countryside is still dotted with covered bridges, some of which date back to the Revolution.

The Urbanites

To optimists it is development. To pessimists it is cancer. Spreading down Interstate 95 from Washington, sending shoots along U. S. Highway 23 to Charlottesville and down I-66 toward the Blue Ridge, an urban sprawl is headed toward the heart of Virginia.

French geographer Jean Gottmann called it *megalopolis*, others name it the East Coast Urban Corridor. In any case, this unbroken mass of humanity begins up around Boston and arcs along the Atlantic seaboard to Washington. And now it has moved beyond, heading inexorably into Virginia.

"It's incredible," says James C. Ruehrmund, editor of *Virginia Facts and Figures*, a state publication. "Fairfax County in northern Virginia changes faster than any other place I've ever lived. Every time I come back there's a new office, a new apartment complex. I have to look twice and think, 'was that there?' The building just fit in because it was surrounded by so much other development.

"I lived about 10 miles outside of Fairfax in 1967. Now my high school friends have had to move 10 or more miles farther out for some open space. That's 20 miles outside of the city for some elbow room.

"I was driving down Interstate 95 and my feeling was, 'Gosh, this is like driving on Broad Street [in Richmond] at rush hour. Washington has grown into Fairfax county into Prince William County. It's just a matter of time before Washington joins Fredericksburg and before Fredericksburg joins Richmond. My bet is that it will happen within the next 20 years. People live mid-way between the urban centers now and think nothing of commuting. My general feeling is that these areas are being drawn together."

A look at the counties running south from Washington shows the swelling of populations.

	1960	1980	2000
Spotsylvania City 13,819	13,819	31,000	62,000
Stafford City 17,000	17,000	38,000+	66,000
Prince William City 41,000	41,000	146,000	257,000

And the heart of the northern Virginia urban expanse bloated from 601,000 in 1960 to more than 1 million in 1978, burying acre upon acre of Virginia countryside beneath gas stations, shopping malls and housing developments.

"The small towns, farms and rolling pastureland of Spotsylvania and Stafford Counties are disappearing faster than in any other area in the state as newcomers continue to flock to the country" stated a UPI report on Virginia's changing cities. And the head of the area's planning commission has said that there is nothing locals can do about the trend but try and cope with it.

The major question facing Virginia today, according to historian Louis D. Rubin, is "how to control and direct urban and industrial development, without jeopardizing natural resources and the environment." In the face of tidal forces moving urbanization forward in all corners of the state, that's a tall order.

In view of this, New Yorkers have begun to think of Richmond as the natural terminus of the urban corridor, not Washington. John McPhee, of *The New Yorker*, has named Boston and Richmond as the true anchors for "an unbroken city" that will one day cover the East Coast. Some uplanders even feel the urban corridor turns left at Richmond and heads straight on to Norfolk.

This urban explosion has unalterably changed the Virginia perspective. A generation ago Fredricksburg lay one-half way between Washington and Richmond. Now it is all but swallowed by the gobbling growth of D.C. suburbs. The concentration of population in the urban corridor has acted like a magnet dragging Virginia attention away from the hills, farms and waters, toward the imposing structures of megalopolis. Washington's influence on Virginia has grown with each new suburb that has been built.

Many would describe this development as expansion, but most Virginians see it as invasion. They note that the root of the growth doesn't lie in expansion within Virginia, but outside of it. Virginia is receiving the spillage from Washington and from New York exiles, who have fled madhouse Manhattan but want to remain a quick plane ride away.

As University of Virginia law professor A. E. Dick Howard noted in his book *Virginia's Urban Corridor:* "Northern Virginia is what it is largely because of the growth of Washington, D.C. Similarly, on both sides of Hampton Roads military bases and other government operations are mainstays of the area's economy. Nowhere else in Virginia is the federal government in such a pivotal position to influence the development and solution of area problems."

Because of this many fear that the northern federal influence zone and the Tidewater zone will meet right around Richmond, forming a strip of governmental fiefdom right through the heart of the state. For years Virginia resisted the growing influence of urban areas. Only in 1971 did reapportionment reflect in the legislature the trend of city domination in Virginia life. To further illustrate, up until the last few sessions, northern Virginia legislators had extreme difficulty getting measures for their area taken seriously down in Richmond. Northern Virginia troubles were seen as Washington's problem, not Virginia's and were dealt with only begrudgingly.

Although Virginians like the idea of economic improvement, new jobs and new amenities, they have trouble abiding the loss of traditional life-styles that comes with "progress."

A case in point is Rockingham County where Coors Beer considered opening its first East Coast brewery. "Once there is the possibility of major new development in a place like that," says James Ruehrmund, "the people there want to keep things the way they always have been. The people are glad to see growth and development if it's going to mean jobs, but they don't want to see their lives changed or their taxes raised."

Rockingham's claim to fame, prior to Coors' interest has been that it has more dairy cows than any other county. This extremely rural outpost also had its share of turkey and chicken farms. The local folk knew the brewery meant jobs, but they still didn't like it.

They were afraid the outside money from the brewery would jack up wages, making it impossible to afford farm help. No one would want to work on a poultry farm if they could get ten dollars an hour to work in a nice clean brewery. Plus, many of the Rockingham citizens were rock-ribbed Southern Baptists who didn't take kindly to the thought of becoming known as Virginia's beer makers.

"They don't want people from other counties or states," Ruehrmund states. "They want their small, nice community to be the same. You'll find the same attitude in Fredericksburg, Richmond and exurban counties like Hanover."

The worst part of Virginia's urban expansion for many rural residents, is the bulk of the growth occurring not in center cities, but in the diminishing rural land on the outskirts of town. Virginia cities are developing a doughnut look—with rings of suburbs around old, stagnant city centers, expanding steadily outward.

The hearts of Virginia's cities have been around for hundreds of years; they were built to the patterns of different ages; they don't have much available space. But the surrounding counties are virgin turf. Builders and businesses can buy up huge chunks and design them as they please. Homeowners can strive for the Virginia ideal of a country-style life within hailing distance of a city.

So, instead of Richmond or Norfolk or Fredericksburg getting taller or more densely populated, they remain much the same. The impact hits like a shock wave through the more distant little towns, overwhelming resorts, general stores, country gas stations, farms, ranches, ponds, streams, two-lane roads and generations of rural living.

The change is sudden, too. In Loudon County, the current edge of Washington's creep southward, the shift can literally be seen on either side of twisting country lanes. On the north end is a chock-a-block condo complex, small living units canted so the maximum density can be reached. A 7-Eleven half built on the corner. A swimming pool behind a high wire fence. Little signs with arrows pointing out how to find your way to the Interstate.

On the south side stand fields. Crooked wood fences. Leafy windbreaks. Tractors and plows. Old cars up on blocks and fishing boats in the front yards. Houses way back off the road in groves of old trees.

The old style is doomed and the new exurban pattern is inevitably taking over, but the people who stand and watch it approaching, development by development don't like it one bit.

By the same token, Virginia's older cities feel abandoned, like the older sister at the ball who can't find anyone to dance with. The new lively exurban counties get all the attention, all the new business, all the new clout. The cities get the problems. They provide many of the services and amenities. And they get saddled with most of the poor.

This has led to another bitter squabble emanating from urban Virginia—annexation. The cities need middle-class tax dollars and new land if they want to expand. They can't manufacture it on the crowded old acres of the existing cities, so they annex hunks of the developing suburbs. As might be expected, the counties and the annexed homeowners don't always like this tactic. In fact, they've been howling about it to the state legislature and anyone else who'll listen. A surly, uneasy truce has been worked out to

soothe cities with state money and protect growing counties from annexation, but the smell of battle still hangs over the issue and political blood will almost certainly still be shed.

The flip side of annexation concerns the inner cities' paranoia about the expanding Interstate Highway system. I-95 has been the conduit for urban expansion into Virginia. The growth has run right along both sides of the giant East Coast highway. And, Catch-22 style, growth spawns more growth. Soon, I-95 will expand to six lanes over the entire distance from Petersburg to Washington.

In addition, the possibility of circumferential beltways being added to the main thrust of the interstate is a real worry to city dwellers, especially Richmonders. Already Washington is girded by a huge beltway, which has spurred expansion of suburbs far out into the once pristine Virginia hills. A new spur line to I-66, running directly from western Virginia to Washington, may push exurbia almost to Harpers Ferry. Richmond doesn't yet have a circumferential highway, but it will soon. And the city and counties are fighting viciously about where the beltway should go and what the city should get in reparations for all that diverted traffic and business. The counties for their part, are starting to worry that the outer highways will bring to suburbia all the woes they thought were confined to downtown.

The urban growth has left many Virginians saddened. They see a way of life passing by. They see favorite spots vanishing in a welter of house frames and new sewer lines. They watch the approaching city like a harvest-time farmer who suspiciously eyes a thunderstorm headed his way. Neither likes what he sees, but feels he can do nothing about it.

Once I stopped at a gas station along Route 1 near Fredricksberg. At one time, Route 1 was the main link between Richmond and Washington, a comfortable, tree-lined road, that followed the natural slope of the land. Then, I-95 opened. Now, the only time Route 1 gets much traffic is when the Interstate is utterly snarled. The drivers are late and surly. They chafe at the stop lights.

The gas station I stopped at was small and old, as was the fellow who ran it. He came out, wiping a greasy rag between bony hands, and performed the necessary business with the pumps and dipstick, then he leaned against the car to shoot the breeze a minute. I told him I often took Route 1 because I found it much more relaxing than the Interstate.

"Well, that's surely true enough," he said, "but that don't matter anymore. Everything is speed and crowding—banging against each other."

He pointed to a ridge that loomed over the Interstate about half-a-mile away. The ridge top had been scalped and houses were rising like warts from the bald spot. "Now will you look at that. Those are Washington people going to live up there. They'll bring Washington money and Washington problems with them. They'll want to know why we don't have in the stores what Washington stores have. And we'll get it. They'll gripe about the roads being narrow and curvy so we'll straighten 'em. They'll get upset by the sounds of the deer rifles, and sure enough there'll be somethin' done to take the fun out of that, too.

"I don't have nuthin' against city folks," he said, "other than that I wish like the Dickens they'd stay in the city, instead of comin' out here."

There are, of course, two valid sides to the question of Virginia urbanization. Northern Virginians will point with pride to the fact that many Virginia greats have come from their ranks. They will also note the cultural benefits they've brought to the state such as Wolf Trap, one of the nation's leading summer concert areas. And, they'll say quite correctly that the highways are clogged on Fridays with Virginians headed *north* to partake of the benefits of the area they deride the rest of the week.

They will also bring up money. Northern Virginia generates it. It has become a high-class headquarters center, one gleaming office after another ranging along the highways toward Washington. It also houses one of the major outposts of American tourist trade—oldtown Alexandria—which attracts bundles of tax money and profits to the Commonwealth.

The counter argument goes that, while these benefits are welcome, they are overshadowed by accompanying problems and by the dangerous un-Virginianness of the new city dwellers.

These people are transient, it is said. They come and go too quickly to put down roots. The famous Virginia aura doesn't have time to take hold. They move in, they change things a bit, then leave. A new crew follows and changes things a little more. These people see Washington as being forward and the rest of Virginia as being backward.

The quintessential example of the strangeness of the new urbanism to the rest of Virginia life is Crystal City in Arlington. Sandwiched between National Airport and a rundown stretch of Route 1, Crystal City rises abruptly among rail yards and old flop houses. It is a starkly modern, hermetically sealed community of several dozen glass-and-steel towers. These contain offices, apartments, hotels and all the basic services and amenities needed to live a busy, socially active life.

The entire complex is connected by underground malls. Going outside is an option. As a result, the streets of Crystal City are peculiarly quiet, even when they are full of cars. They lack life. Inside, of course, there is life aplenty—but not life in a recognizable Virginia form. To go out of one's way to be insulated from nature strikes most Virginians as perverse.

Apart from the ganglia of northern Virginia, and in spite of reluctance toward change, urban areas are increasing their hold on Virginia life. Virginia cities used to be like overgrown small towns. Not too exciting, but friendly and easily understood. Now, as they steadily grow, the commonwealth's urban centers are getting more exciting, but also more complex and contentious. They are finding that they are not immune to the urban ills of cities everywhere.

Crime is rising. Drugs are about. Sedate places like Richmond have had to deal with a mushroom growth of shady massage parlors and out-call red-light services. Inner-city neighborhoods are getting old and dilapidated. Downtowns are struggling, while suburbs keep eating up more outlying land.

Until recently, it could be argued that there existed no such thing as an urban Virginian. There were Virginians who lived in cities, but they never had to develop the thick skin, the detached attitude, the suspicious nature of a true urbanite. They didn't have to construct coping mechanisms for living in town. Now, they do.

Still, Virginia's cities offer an ambiance of almost European proportions. They are dotted with parks and lakes that people are not afraid to use at night. They offer operas, theater, music and dance of the highest caliber. They have suave entertainment districts on a par with anything offered elsewhere—at prices much more agreeable. And they still feature lots of close-to-the-ground living space. Nowhere, except in northern Virginia do you yet see large numbers of apartment towers. The total separation from nature that comes with true megalopolis hasn't afflicted most of Virginia, yet.

Virginia has an excellent chance, in fact, to help develop a new form of urban living that avoids some of the problems of today's sprawling graffiti-strewn metropoli. At Reston in the north and Brandermill near Richmond, developers and owners have attempted to build new styles of towns. These places have been planned as whole communities from the first instant. No factor in development was left to chance. Stores, homes and offices were situated for the best balance of efficiency and segregation. Recreational facilities were carefully melded into the plan. Natural surroundings were carefully preserved.

To date, both seem to be smash successes and Virginians look upon them as patterns for sensible future growth.

Virginia's cities have benefited from an influx of artistic and literary talent over the past few years. The air age has brought Virginia to New York's doorstep. Many artists and writers, who would have felt pressured to move to New York, now choose to stay in Virginia instead.

"I can have my cake and eat it, too," a Virginia photographer once told me. "I get to live in a great townhouse I could never afford up north. And I'm right near the country, the ocean. The people are much friendlier than in New York and Washington. But if I need to get up there on business, it's no problem. Virginia is as far away as I can get from the big cities and still be in touch."

And, with more young, creative city dwellers, have come better restaurants and more varied night life and generally a more spicy community feeling.

The young professionals who are staying in town rather than heading for the suburbs or bigger cities are also helping to rebuild historic old neighborhoods. In cities all over the state young couples are buying and fixing up the big old houses near the center of town. They, more than any influx of government money, may be responsible for arresting the decay of Virginia city centers.

Virginia's cities have been struggling to save their downtown shopping areas, as well. They have built ultra-modern convention and concert halls to lure suburbanites back into town at night. They've tried turning the downtowns into landscaped malls and holding special activities there. Still, the attrition that seems to be striking so many American downtowns continues. One by one stores light out for sleek new suburban locations, leaving behind a garish residue of steak joints, pool halls, girlie parlors and second-rate merchandise outlets.

Virginia's downtowns are far from dead, though. And efforts continue on all fronts to revitalize them. If a saving grace exists, it's that Virginians really don't seem to want their downtowns to go. Citizens I've talked with in other parts of the country apparently don't give a damn one way or the other about their towns, but Virginians do care. And so, in time, they may come up with a plan that works.

Urbanization in Virginia has brought problems and new potential, but most of all it has brought variety. For better or worse, Virginia cities are a heck of a lot more interesting than they used to be.

On a clear spring day in the country south of Dulles Airport, a young girl, her pony tail flying out behind her, jumps her horse in the paddock beside the family home. Across the road, a begrimed worker leans on a shovel and watches her, while his colleagues dig the foundation for a new shopping plaza.

In the Norfolk bus terminal at midnight one winter night sit: three black sailors talking a blue streak; a short plump woman in a sari with a baby sleeping in her lap; a young hairy fellow wearing a floppy hat and reading a copy of *Walden II* with his feet propped up on a worn guitar case; a middle-aged man in a suit a size too small with a patterned shirt underneath; a well-dressed white woman chain smoking and constantly looking around; a huge black grandmother whose body cascades off the chair in all directions; two clean-cut intense young people with the shiny-eyed faces of cultists; an extensive family with a Spanish look—migrant workers, perhaps; a tall thin sam in a dark pinstriped suit, reading a copy of *Barrons*.

In Jarrells Truck Plaza on I-95, the behemoth road buggies slumber in a city-sized parking lot. Inside, on a balcony overlooking the cavernous public cafeteria, Big John Trimble, king of the trucker disc jockeys, stares down on his flock through a large glass window. Some truckers come in and wave, John waves back and beckons them to his studio. He'll put them on the air, ask about their wives, sweethearts, hauls and problems. "Big John may work for the radio," says one of them, "but he's a trucker at heart."

A thin black boy struts down Broad Street in Richmond carrying a radio the size of a suitcase. It blares forth a thumping beat and unintelligible music. When people glare at him, the young man stops and turns the radio up.

In Alexandria, a dainty old lady with white gloves blithely strolls down the street with her flouncing granddaughter in jeans, sweatshirt and hair to her waist.

In downtown Danville, a well turned-out fellow walks up and down preaching the Gospel to anyone close enough to hear. Around the corner, a student with his hair tied back hands out political pamphlets. Both get about the same response. Moonies, like smiling butterflies flit from person to person handing out flowers and collecting cash at a Roanoke mall . . .

What's happening in Virginia's cities may not be entirely salutary, but it's certainly far from dull. It may even turn out to be enriching.

A symbol of new urbanism: northern Virginia's computerized metro subways.

Riding the "Rebel Yell" at King's Dominion.

Big John Trimble, rides the airwaves from Virginia to truckers all over
the continent.

Youngsters seem to come of age more quickly in urban areas.

An unidentified supporter of the Equal Rights Amendment shouts during a rally at the Capitol Building in Richmond. (UPI)

The latest life styles no longer dawdle on their way into Virginia.

Tender loneliness in Richmond, where a Jefferson Hotel pensioner strokes one of the birds he tends for companionship.

Richmond's marathon draws thousands of runners from all over the country.

Urban Virginia offers big city amenities such as Richmond's professional
hockey franchise.

213

Urban Virginia offers big city amenities such as Richmond's professional hockey franchise.

The Children

It's not that Virginia children are better than those elsewhere, they're just luckier.

A New York child knows only the city; an Iowa child only the land. But a Virginia child can know both, with the mountains and ocean thrown in for good measure.

And a Virginia child has the advantage of being born into the strongest, most enduring tradition in America. Whether in the country or in a town, in the Appalachians or along the shore, an Old Dominion youngster is buttressed by the frame of widely accepted custom and purpose that motivates his community and family.

They are mercurial, quixotic, joyous, frenetic, happy, devastated, sly, precious, precocious and peeving as children always are. But they are more. In Virginia, children are the recipients of a generations-old trust. They must carry on the Virginia way. The sense of specialness engendered in the days of Jefferson must be passed on to them. The synthesis of history and possibility that forms the central flow of Virginia civilization must be catalyzed into a new generation through the children.

And Virginia children have that unequalled head start in life that Woodrow Wilson talked about. The extra step on the rest of their generation that comes from Virginia's values and virtues, the courage to steer by the stars and not the ground.

227

Photography Credits

Photography was an integral part of the conception and execution of this book. Two men in particular performed magnificently in gathering images of their home state. Lee Brauer of Richmond and Thomas Daniel of Tidewater traveled all over Virginia, allowed their businesses to suffer, and waited ever so patiently to see the results of all their effort. They took most of the photos in *The Virginians*.

However, as the overseer of the project, I wanted it to convey more than two views of Virginia's appearance and appeal. So I have included photos from other sources that I felt expressed a particularly valuable point, or which I thought especially handsome.

Here is a listing of who took which picture:

BLACK AND WHITE PHOTOS:

p. 25 Lee Brauer (LB)
p. 26 Taylor Dabney
p. 27 LB
p. 28 UPI
p. 29 LB
p. 30 LB
p. 31 LB
p. 32 Thomas Daniel (TD)
p. 33 LB
p. 34 LB
p. 35 UPI
p. 51 Taylor Dabney
p. 52 LB
p. 53 Taylor Dabney
p. 54 LB
p. 55 Taylor Dabney
p. 71 TD
p. 72 TD
p. 73 TD
p. 74 UPI
p. 75 Virginia State Travel Service
p. 76 *Richmond Magazine*
p. 77 UPI
p. 78 UPI
p. 79 TD
p. 80 Virginia State Travel Service
p. 81 UPI
p. 97 *Richmond Magazine*
p. 98 TD
p. 99 TD
p. 100 Taylor Dabney
p. 101 Taylor Dabney

p. 102 TD
p. 103 TD
p. 104 UPI
p. 105 TD
p. 120 R.V. Fuschetto/Photo Researchers
p. 121 UPI
p. 122 UPI
p. 123 UPI
p. 124 G. C. Kenny/Image Bank
p. 125 LB
p. 126 LB
p. 127 LB
p. 128 UPI
p. 129 UPI
p. 146 TD
p. 147 TD
p. 148 TD
p. 149 TD
p. 150 UPI
p. 151 TD
p. 152 UPI
p. 153 LB
p. 154 *Richmond Magazine*
p. 155 UPI
p. 156 TD
p. 157 Taylor Dabney
p. 173 LB
p. 174 LB
p. 175 Brian Seed/Black Star
p. 176 TD
p. 177 TD

Index

(Bold face numbers refer to pages with photographs)

231